SEE CHANGE CLEARLY

SEE CHANGE CLEARLY

LEVERAGING ADVERSITY TO SHARPEN YOUR VISION AND BUILD RESILIENT TEAMS

JACOB GREEN

LIONCREST
PUBLISHING

SEE CHANGE CLEARLY
Leveraging Adversity to Sharpen Your
Vision and Build Resilient Teams

ISBN   978-1-5445-1339-3 *Paperback*
        978-1-5445-1338-6 *Ebook*

PORTION OF THE PROCEEDS

A portion of the proceeds from this book will go to Coastline's Acquired Brain Injury Program scholarships and services: a program which helped me see change clearly.

IN MEMORY OF

In memory of Brianne Catherine Schwantes—advocate, friend, and a model of compassionate authenticity. We will continue to remember one of your favorite quotes from Grandma Eileen:

"No one should be taught to be afraid of life. Bad things are going to happen, and we'll just deal with them one at a time."

I still wear my safety pin.

CONTENTS

INTRODUCTION

"There's a tide in the affairs of men which, taken at the flood, leads on to fortune; Omitted, all the voyage of their life is bound in shallows and in miseries. On such a full sea are we now afloat, and we must take the current when it serves, or lose our ventures."
—WILLIAM SHAKESPEARE, *JULIUS CAESAR*, ACT IV

Greg Devereaux was quoting Shakespeare and poetically telling me to "take the leap." It was the third time in as many weeks that the city manager of Ontario, California, had asked me to his office. Each time, he'd offered me a promotion to the position of Administrative Director in the police department, which I turned down each time because I loved my job at the Ontario Fire Department. Greg remained silent after quoting Shakespeare. I asked if I could go speak to my boss, Fire Chief Chris Hughes.

Not only was I surprised that the city manager would resort to a perfectly recited quote from Shakespeare, but I was also wary of leaving the stability and support that I benefitted from at the fire department. Just a few years prior my wife had battled cancer, and the men and women of Ontario Fire supported us through each day. I loved the job and loved the fire family. I walked across the parking lot from City Hall to Chris' office and went in without knocking—our three-year relationship rebuilding parts of the department allowed for this.

"Greg's quoting Shakespeare. What am I supposed to do?" I asked.

"You know what you have to do," Chris said. He was right. I made the long journey back across the parking lot and upstairs to Greg's office and said, "I spoke to Chris. I'm in. When do I start?"

NEVER READY, SLIGHTLY TERRIFIED

Shakespeare's words hang framed over my desk, and I look at them every day. They remind me that no one ever feels ready for the big changes in life, yet the leap is worth taking. Change, however painful, can bring great rewards and growth. I didn't feel ready to get married. I didn't feel ready to buy my first house. I didn't feel ready to have children. I didn't feel ready for the promotion and opportunity Greg offered me. I'm glad I did all of those things, despite feeling unprepared.

Most people who start a new job or pursue a new opportunity feel unprepared, overwhelmed, and even terrified at the beginning. They think they feel ready to take on new responsibilities and do something different. It's more likely that what they are feeling is a need for *change*, a need for a new environment and new challenges, which is not the same as feeling ready to move up the ladder into a new supervisory or management position.

It's important to recognize the difference between needing a change and feeling ready for change. When a person enters a new position or takes on challenging responsibilities—especially as a new manager or supervisor—rather than feeling overcome with joy, they may feel overwhelmed by a perceived lack of skills and the inability to handle the scope of the new position and opportunity, like I did. Ellen Hendriksen, PhD, a clinical psychologist at Boston University's Center for Anxiety and Related Disorders, says leaders may be suffering from "imposter syndrome" when they experience feelings of self-doubt, insecurity, or fraudulence, in spite of having received recognition for achievements and being called to take on bigger responsibilities by their organization as a result.

I know this to be true because every time I've been promoted, regardless of the position, when I tried on the hat of the new role and envisioned myself there, I felt overwhelmed by a sense of incompetency and unreadiness. I felt terrified on the first day of my new job in the Ontario Police Department, much like I have on the first day of every new job I've accepted. Not only did I have to learn where the bathrooms were, find people to eat lunch with, and navigate a different set of office politics, I had to prove my value to a new boss and new colleagues.

NO PLACE TO GO BUT UP

Although the pay raise and the opportunity for professional growth in the police department position were enticing, I couldn't imagine not working for Chris Hughes and the rest of the fire department team. Chris was the epitome of a leader: decisive, stable, and humble, and every day was about growth. He was tough on me, had high expectations, and regularly pointed out my blind spots; but this directness allowed for rapid personal and professional growth and a sense that he was investing in me.

Three months into working at Ontario, Chris asked me to represent the fire department on a panel at a public event. The position on the panel next to the mayor and city manager rightly belonged to Chris, but he didn't need the recognition, nor did he like to be in the limelight. The phrase he often used, which I have repeated on more than one occasion myself, was "successful, not famous." He wanted the fire department to shine, and he liked to give others the opportunity to contribute.

I was on call 24/7 as the entry level disaster analyst and public information officer for the department, and I went out on calls at all hours of the night, any day of the week. I couldn't get enough of my job. I felt there was value and importance in what I was doing, I knew who I was and why I was doing it, and I was serving a group of professionals that I looked up to. Legendary speaker Jim Rohn is credited with saying that we are "the average of the five people we spend time with." I was surrounded by hundreds of people on a daily basis who I looked up to and who pushed me to perform at a higher level; I was certain I would work at the fire department for the duration of my career.

From the time I began in the fire department, I had admired Greg from afar. With so few opportunities to interact with him directly due to my entry level status, I made up excuses every chance I got to get a closer understanding of his success. I would tell Chris, "For my grad school assignment, I am supposed to interview the city manager about leadership." (The assignment would actually be about accounting principles, but it didn't matter.) With Chris's permission, I'd schedule an appointment and slide into Greg's office for my fifteen-minute appointment. Ninety minutes later, I'd emerge inspired, energized, and with a little more insight about the challenges of the chief executive.

Greg, an unwavering city manager, saw a future beyond the fire department for me. Saying "no" to his offer wasn't an option.

When a person has been in the same job and starts to plateau, that person ultimately reaches a decision point: stay comfortable with boredom, seek an internal promotion, or pursue a better position at a different organization. The itch for upward mobility can be stronger than the practicality of what that upward mobility looks and feels like. Promotions are exciting, and new managers are usually thrilled when that offer comes, but leadership books don't talk about the paradigm shift promotions represent. When the Champagne corks have popped and the celebration for the promotion is over, the next feeling is often total overwhelm, anxiety, and a sense of self-doubt and impending failure. From one day to the next, in the transition from the old position to the new one, an identity crisis happens. When I moved from the fire department to the police department, I was no longer the expert to whom people came for answers; I was the new kid on the block, with little credit for past performance.

Most humans have deep-seated insecurities about who they are. Because of our innate need and desire to fit in with a crowd and seek external validation, we look up to leaders and feel valued when colleagues depend on us. Change and new environments bring those insecurities to the surface. When Greg told me that I was ready for a supervisory opportunity, my initial response was, "Are you sure?"

REAPING THE FORTUNES

Many new managers question their worthiness when it comes to being ready for a promotion. Likewise, leaders who are asked to tackle a difficult situation, such as revamping a department or firing an employee that isn't performing, may want to shirk their responsibilities because they don't believe they're up to the task. An estimated seventy percent of people will experience at least one episode of impostor syndrome in their lives.

When they assume that role, all of their deep-seated fears and anxieties materialize immediately, because their surroundings are different. The new position becomes a quest to create a sense of familiarity and grounding in order to move forward successfully within the new challenge.

By incorporating a series of strategies and techniques at

the right time, however, leaders can reap all of the fortunes that Brutus predicted as he led his men into the final battles of war. By taking the leap, despite paralyzing anxiety, leaders can experience great growth and fortune, which is exactly what happened to me in the Ontario Police Department and all subsequent career opportunities that followed. If I consider where I began, I realize my fortune and growth is even greater than I, or anyone else, ever imagined, and is a direct result of those who believed in me despite my limitations.

BRAIN SCHOOL

I suffered a myriad of injuries, including a traumatic brain injury at eighteen, followed by almost three years of full-time physical and cognitive rehabilitation, and years more of ongoing treatment. At the sixth month mark, when I desperately wanted to return to the University of California, Berkeley where I had been a student, doctors told me I should think about trade school. Instead, after years of relearning how to learn, I applied the strategies I learned in brain school to obtain bachelor's and master's degrees and went on to apply the brain school lessons in everyday life, including the workplace.

This book is about navigating change in the workplace. I will show you how these brain school strategies can help anyone stepping up to a new work challenge and how those lessons can help companies navigate change and build resilient teams ready for any crisis. One of the best examples of sudden change in the workplace is the first day on the job or the new promotion. I'll make many references to that as a great example, although this book will help you and your team face any change, regardless of whether you are new to your position or a tenured pro.

The overwhelming chaos and confusion I felt after my brain injury is not so different from the apprehension and trepidation I felt on the first day of a new job. I use strategies from brain school to lead teams in my organization, and I share these strategies when I speak to companies throughout the country about change management.

New managers and long-time leaders alike can use these strategies to manage change in their organizations. The steps I present are:

- **Gain self-awareness:** knowing oneself is key to leading others. I recommend the AEM-Cube tool to learn about your own strengths and weaknesses as well as those of team members.
- **Get to know those around you:** I share specific questions managers can ask their boss, their peers, and everyone on the team to begin building or improving relationships.
- **Identify gaps:** brain school taught me the importance

of assessing a problem before trying to solve it. I share my method for separating problems from emergencies and ways to identify the true issue at hand.

- **Build compensatory techniques:** as the backbone of dealing with a brain injury, compensatory techniques are the secret sauce to solving problems. I walk through specific techniques I use for day-to-day tasks and the process for building compensatory techniques for any type of challenge.

- **Create an authentic environment:** authenticity happens when everyone is open about their own challenges. I discuss the ten specific benefits and outcomes an authentic environment enables.

- **Lean on others:** being responsible for change or entering a new position is stressful and can feel lonely. Learning to lean on others is a sign of strength, not weakness.

It's not every day you hear words like "gaps" and "compensatory techniques" used in a business book. You might need to read more slowly and unpack the message to see how it applies to you. If you're confused, welcome to the world of brain injuries. When you have a brain injury or a complex challenge at work, you might be disoriented so you have to uncover all the layers, look from different perspectives, and ask different people for feedback. If the answers were easy I wouldn't have written a book about them.

I've been immersed in public service since age fourteen. In my darkest hour of recovery from my brain injury, I dreamed about one day being able to help others navigate catastrophic change and create some value out of my experiences. By revealing some of my most challenging moments, I hope readers see how I use what I learned, and more importantly, how they can use what I learned to face change in the workplace and create success. Whether they're entering their first management role, or facing crisis in the workplace, the tools in this book allow leaders to figure out where to begin to address change, how to approach each day, and ultimately build resilient teams.

CHAPTER 1

THE SUBWAY

When I was a freshman at the University of California, Berkeley, I worked as a Berkeley Guide. The program's mission was to keep downtown Berkeley safer, which meant helping businesses deal with difficult customers or showing tourists the way to Chez Panisse.

On rainy evenings, Berkeley Guides did one of two things: they sat in the local movie theater or hung out in one of the Bay Area Rapid Transit subway stations (known by locals as BART stations) to stay dry. When it began to rain on a Friday night in February 1998, Sander, my Berkeley Guide partner for the evening, and I opted for the Shattuck BART Station.

A few seconds after we stepped onto the down escalator, a heavy-set woman ran toward us from below—up the down escalator—her shopping bags whipping and flailing against the bodies of the crowd headed down to the track. She screamed, "Get out of my way!" and pushed my skinny eighteen-year-old frame aside. I would have been wise to turn and follow her, but instead Sander and I continued our descent into the abyss of the Shattuck station.

As we got closer to the bottom, I noticed something was wrong. This was not the normal noise and bustling of commuters returning to Berkeley from San Francisco or East Bay folks headed to the city for a Friday night outing. This was chaos; people were running in random directions and screaming. The crowd parted like the Red Sea, giving me a direct sight line to the ticket booth twenty feet in front of me. In that moment, I saw the cause of the cacophony.

Inside the glass booth, a tall, robust man, sweating profusely, eyes bulging white with rage, bellowed repeatedly above the din of the crowd, "Give me the money! Give me the money! Give me the money!" all the while picking up anything he could—keyboards, phones, monitors, pencil cups—and hurling them down. He then began opening and slamming the door of the booth, causing the entire glass cube to shudder. Papers swirled around the booth, which took on a surreal resemblance to the wind tunnel money game. Two female ticket agents shrunk against the glass wall, holding their hands up to protect their faces.

As I took in the details of the scene, I saw one of the agents had a red phone in her hand. A red phone calls one of two people: the police or Batman. In that moment, it didn't matter who she called, but that call had to go through. I wanted to distract the man long enough for the agent to make the call on the red phone. Then the police would show up, arrest the man, and everyone could get back to their Friday evening. As I stepped closer to the booth, I turned to Sander and said, "Call the police." Sander, who described himself as an international arms trader and martial arts ninja, had the same white bulging eyes as the man in the booth and was frozen in his spot, useless as a gum wrapper in a moment when two heads and two sets of hands would have been better than one.

I yelled as loud as I could, "Sir, hey, calm down man. Get out of the booth. Come talk to me." It was the only plan I could think of and he listened. I weighed all of 118 pounds soaking wet, and the six-foot-four man stepped out of the booth. Like a stuntman, he jumped over the pony gate and ran straight at me, reached behind his back, pulled something out, and began striking the side of my head with it. I put my hands out in front of me in a marginal attempt to block his vision and turned my head to lessen the blows.

A significant phrase from the police explorer training I'd taken as a teenager kicked in from the recesses of my brain: "Stay on your feet. If you go to the ground, you're dead." My singular goal was to stay on my feet.

After the fourth or fifth blow, I blacked out. My next memory is standing in the midst of the janitorial supplies, using the yellow bucket and mops as a barrier between me and the thug. I took the "position of interrogation," again recalling my police explorer training, outstretching my left hand to block the man's line of vision, and shifting my right hip, where my gun would have been if I'd had one, backward to keep it away from my assailant. That night the only weapons I carried were a pencil and a calculator, but the interrogation technique training helped me block some of the blows to my face. I bobbed and swerved, somewhat successfully avoiding the swings he launched through the mops. All the while the mantra, "Stay on my feet. Stay on my feet. Stay on my feet." ran through my head.

While my assailant and I were dancing with the mops, I glimpsed another off-duty Berkeley Guide, Lashawn (Shawn) Nolen in the crowd. Shawn yelled at my assailant, who turned and ran toward him, and Shawn, who had grown up on the streets of Berkeley, started running away. My last thought before blacking out was, "If Shawn is running away from this guy, this is bad."

When I came to, I was on the street above the BART

station, at the corner of Shattuck and University, just a block north. The police officer to my right was pointing her pepper spray and yelling "Get your hands up," to the thug who had chased Shawn up to the street level. She put handcuffs on him and said the paramedics were on their way to take me to the emergency room. The next few hours were a blur. During one of my waking moments, the ER staff conducted a strength and coordination neurological test, which I passed. They sent me back to my dorm room with a diagnosis of a concussion and a hematoma, as they noted a golf ball sized knot behind my left ear and told me, "The swelling will decrease. You're fine."

I believed them. I was eighteen. What did I know?

WHO AM I?

My entire scholastic life I'd been able to hold my own. I wasn't at the top of my class, but I had figured out how to be a successful student. In the first months of college, I'd developed a mastery of the lecture hall, taking copious notes and acing exams. My peers and I had cracked the code of understanding what the professor was looking for and how to execute it. As long as I knew the rules, the perspective of the professor, and the average performance of my peers, I could thrive in the classroom, and I did for many years prior. Then, overnight, all the ways in which I was able to absorb and process information, identify with my peers, and understand my environment were gone.

After being attacked, I lost all my coping skills and control over my environment. Every movement, every backpack opening, every whisper distracted me from focusing on the professor. My notebooks, which were filled with lecture notes up to February 5th, were empty after February 6th. My grades plummeted from A's and B's to straight F's. My anxiety soared to severe levels, and I felt an overwhelming sense of inferiority compared to my peers, who continued to operate and attend class without apparent difficulty, while my good-student identity was gone.

After three weeks of constant headaches, vomiting, and missing classes, my mom came to Berkeley from Southern California to help me. She spent years as a social worker in a pediatric neuro unit at a large hospital and knew I was experiencing some of the same symptoms she'd witnessed on the ward. After months of trying to get insurance authorization for testing and treatment, scans confirmed a traumatic brain injury, occipital neuralgia, and a whole host of visual impairments. Diagnosis in hand, I had no choice but to drop out of college and begin my long road to recovery.

BRAIN SCHOOL LESSON NO. 1: SELF-AWARENESS

Much, if not all, of a person's knowledge and capabilities is altered when brain injury occurs. Humans build their self-identity and self-awareness on what they know and what they can do. After a brain injury, their self-identity needs to be rebuilt and self-awareness relearned. Brain injury school, or rehabilitation, gives those who have suffered a brain injury a PhD in self-awareness so that when they're out in the world, they truly can be in touch with their strengths and apply those strengths to new careers and new lives. At the same time, they need to identify remaining deficits or gaps.

After six months of full-time rehabilitation with a team of speech therapists, occupational therapists, physical therapists, and neuro-psychologists, the doctors sat me down and told me that while I was medically stable, I wasn't functioning well enough to return to college. The next step, they said, was intensive cognitive rehabilitation; learning how to learn again. The best program in California was the Coastline Acquired Brain Injury in Costa Mesa (now in Newport Beach). I packed up my college life and relocated to a small studio apartment within walking distance of my new, two-year cognitive retraining school in Southern California, some 400 miles away from my former college life.

I first met my brain injury school companions in an elementary classroom better suited to third graders than adults. Realizing this was going to be my home for the next two years, I observed and categorized the people in the room.

There was Sally, the elementary school teacher who wore her hair in a tight bun and radiated kindness and compassion; Iris, a fifty-five-year-old psychotherapist, who had deep, gazing eyes and an intense interaction style that made me feel like I was lying on her couch for psychoanalysis; Keith, a six-foot-eight dentist who had survived his suicide attempt; and Ellen, a lively redhead whose booming voice could be heard in the corridor long before she entered the classroom.

Then I saw George. Despite his tall, strong, fifty-something build, George walked with a cane and struggled with one side of his body that didn't work properly. Although he sat in the back of the classroom, his presence was often felt. His cane fell and clattered on the floor every few minutes, and he raised his hand every twenty seconds. His first question was, "What did you say your name was, teacher?"

The teacher replied, "Kathy."

George continued unabashedly, "Well, you have a beautiful dress on today, Kathy. Quite the looker!"

Without missing a beat, Kathy thanked George, and then asked the class how we felt about his comment. Iris, having the advantage of her psychotherapist training, raised her hand and said, "You know, George, while you were trying to come from a good place, you may have made an inappropriate comment that made the teacher feel uncomfortable. But it's okay, George. We're obviously in this thing together."

George's ire rose. He angrily defended his comment as an intended compliment and then insulted Iris and a few others in the classroom, pointing out all of our less-than-desirable physical features. Iris's nose, Keith's bald spot, my youth. George's behavior would provide plenty of learning opportunities during our two years together. Kathy used this episode to introduce the concept of self-awareness and emotional intelligence. During the two years of brain school, we used Daniel Goleman's seminal text, *Emotional Intelligence,* to relearn how to read while relearning self-awareness, to understand who we were, our place in the world, and how to interact with those around us.

REBUILDING AN IDENTITY

After my brain injury, the person I used to be—the honors student, the public servant—no longer existed. Suddenly, the identity that had served me until the day before was no longer true or stable. I found myself in a new environment. Instead of being surrounded by top-achieving students at UC Berkeley studying international diplomacy, I was surround by brain injury patients on an elementary school campus.

In brain school, the medical professionals, the coaches, and the rehabilitation experts put patients through a journey of re-discovering how they respond to others, how they interact with the outside world, who they are, and who they want to become. I had to learn how to ask new questions of my doctors and my peers to gain self-awareness, to understand how I was being perceived, to identify the strengths and gaps in my abilities, and to build confidence.

For the most part, I had a good idea of how others perceived me. However, I had a damaged sense of self and my identity, and part of rehabilitation and brain injury school for me was the process of re-building my identity. Years later, when I transitioned to new responsibilities at work, the same thing happened: the identity that had served me the day before had to be rebuilt, or at least adjusted.

Regardless of the situation that has brought about uncertainty and change in the workplace, all leaders need to have a defined identity, which enables them to exude confidence. Their confidence, in turn, instills confidence in their team and ensures they follow them through the rough waters of change and uncertainty to reach the calm seas on the other side of the storm.

New managers, on the other hand, have to *rebuild* their identity. When someone asks, "What do you do?" they don't really know because they've just begun. While a promotion is a positive thing, it's still a new change that can provoke anxiety, which can be perceived as weakness and lack of confidence.

MAKING CONNECTIONS

Brain injury school consisted of intensive cognitive retraining, four days a week: memorization techniques, reading comprehension strategies, and relearning how to learn. With college life placed on hold and my prior dream of becoming an international diplomat well out of reach, a major component in re-building my sense of self in brain injury school was the process of seeing how I could reconnect to others and connect to a new life purpose.

Nearly two years into rehabilitation, the brain injury team asked me what I wanted to do with my time that wasn't devoted to doctor appointments and rehab. I said, "I've always wanted to be a Red Cross volunteer." Instead of them saying, "You can't possibly be a Red Cross volunteer," they said, "We don't know whether you're able to do it or not, but if you're excited about the potential of being a Red Cross volunteer, we're willing to go on that journey with you."

I sat with the brain injury team in front of a computer, doing research about what it would take to become a certified Red Cross volunteer. I then went through the process of learning how to call the local Red Cross chapter and enroll in the class. Then I went to the Red Cross training class, armed with tools from the rehab team. The process of getting attached to and excited about something out in the world allayed the feeling of impending doom and gloom that I experienced on a daily basis with my brain injury. After I successfully completed my Red Cross volunteer certification, I felt confident to identify and work toward other goals, like getting my EMT certification, which I ultimately achieved by following the same process.

In the business world, when feelings of overwhelming anxiety and self-doubt surface, a leader can alleviate those feelings through connecting to others and finding the meaning in what she does. Self-doubt is particularly strong when an opportunity is offered that the leader hasn't applied for, which happened for me when Greg offered me the position with the police department, which I described in the introduction. Not only did I love the job I had with the fire department, I felt full of self-doubt and completely unprepared to take on the position.

When I began my police department job, I oversaw multiple divisions, and each required some investment of time in improvement and enhancement. I couldn't tackle everything at once, nor did I have the knowledge base I needed. I felt overwhelmed. The prospect of being responsible for fiscal services and the department's $65 million budget left me a sweaty mess. I concluded that I had a tenured staff in place, and instead I needed to focus some initial effort on an area where I had confidence. I began with the area I knew and enjoyed the most, which was dispatch. The so-called domino effect took place. Making improvements in the dispatch division gave me the confidence, energy, and motivation to take on less familiar and more complicated divisions. I took on larger responsibilities as I became more comfortable and confident in my ability to perform.

I followed the same process after a promotion that I had followed in rehabilitation. The enthusiasm and satisfaction derived from completing one goal provided motivation to move on to the next. Success fuels the ability to engage in areas that may not be so familiar or feel as natural.

When a manager has feelings of self-doubt, one technique to try is identifying elements of the position that are most exciting and engaging. Identify the parts that will be easier to tackle or may be challenging but will provide satisfaction for a job well done.

THE IMPORTANCE OF EMOTIONAL INTELLIGENCE

Leaders, in their earnestness to do a good job—much like George who thought he was giving the teacher a compliment—may act without self-control or the ability to understand the impact of their actions on others.

In *Emotional Intelligence,* Daniel Goleman writes, "The range of what we think and do is limited by what we fail to notice. And because we fail to notice that we fail to notice there is little we can do to change until we notice how failing to notice shapes our thoughts and deeds." Goleman's book is a great resource for a new leader or manager who's looking to gain self-awareness.

A large city in California with close to 2,000 employees hired a new city manager, essentially the CEO of the city. After a short seven days on the job, he fired the top executives, one of whom was extremely talented by most accounts. From the outside looking in, this action seemed impulsive. How, after one week, could a leader know that these veteran executives should be dismissed? And what impact would that impulsive action have on the rest of the organization? Did he consider the anxiety and angst that such a move might cause in the lower levels of the organization? Did he think about the possible exodus that might result when a well-loved leader was let go?

I don't suggest that leaders should avoid firing poor performers. I am suggesting that leaders think about the ramifications aggressive actions may have throughout the organization. New leaders are often hired to repair a struggling team. However, if leaders impulsively impose new policies and philosophies without considering the impact they'll have on the existing environment, they risk bringing down the organization they were brought in to improve.

The leader may be feeling insecure in the new position and make those rapid changes to prove her value to a new boss and colleagues. The leader may be operating in a sense of arrogant bliss, but team members and colleagues will be subject to whatever chaos or reinvention she brings into the workplace.

One of the highest qualities of a person with advanced emotional intelligence is the ability to delay gratification, which is the opposite of impulsiveness. The impulsive leader, who doesn't go through a process of self-awareness and exploration prior to diving into a proper assessment of the problem she's been hired to solve, is a doomed leader. To prevent attrition, new leaders must go through a process of building and ensuring self-awareness and embrace getting in touch with blind spots, challenges, and strengths.

PRACTICING SELF-AWARENESS

Good leadership begins with self-awareness. Self-awareness is apparent in the big and small actions of a leader. For example, when I was promoted to administrative director of the police department, on my first day I could have mandated dispatchers to wear police uniforms instead of polo shirts and slacks, because in my previous department everyone wore uniforms.

A self-aware leader, however, won't come in to a new position and change the uniforms overnight. She's going to open up a discussion by saying things like, "Tell me a little bit about the last time you changed uniforms. Tell me why these uniforms were selected. Do people like the uniforms that they're currently wearing? How many people don't like the uniforms they're currently wearing? Where is the uniform policy? Who wrote the uniform policy? What year was the uniform policy written? How can we take our uniforms to the next level? Who has a say in what uniforms the dispatchers wear? Is this a decision that's ultimately made by the chief of police? Is this a decision that could be made by the police administrative director? Is this a decision that the union has to weigh in on and have ultimate decision-making authority over? Is there something about the uniforms that allows us to do our jobs? Do we go out into the field at all? Do we respond with the SWAT team as dispatchers and therefore have to be identified differently in the field than we do in the dispatch center, and therefore there's a reason why we wear certain uniforms? Was there a major incident or event that led to the particular choice to wear this kind of uniform?"

This may seem like an extreme example, but making fast, aggressive, uninformed changes is how a lot of leaders operate. A leader with a lack of self-awareness may think the absence of uniforms demonstrated an absence of professionalism and displayed sloppiness. She may believe giving dispatchers a uniform would build their sense of identity with the department. By taking the time to ask questions about why previous choices were made, the new leader may discover that dispatchers don't go out in the field. She may learn that six months ago a committee put together the polo and slacks standard because the uniforms were making the dispatchers, who sit for many hours a day, feel physically uncomfortable. They had to untuck their uniform shirts and that looked sloppy.

At multiple times in their careers, leaders need to reevaluate what they believe are their strengths. The tactics that worked in the past may not be the best strategy in the new position. Spending time evaluating internal strengths and weaknesses and building self-awareness of the impact of their actions on this new environment not only saves the new manager from wreaking havoc on what is possibly already a tenuous situation, but also enables those on the team to contribute with their highest potential. Rather than going blindly into a new position, new managers would be wise to take the appropriate time to reflect on their strengths and weaknesses.

FORMER STRENGTHS BECOME WEAKNESSES

Many leaders think the same leadership skills transfer from one position to the next. If they were a successful leader in one situation, they'll be a successful leader in another. This isn't always true. The environment can exacerbate or highlight strengths and weaknesses.

Before my injury, I embodied academic confidence and focus, which I lost in an instant that night in the Berkeley BART station. In reality, those that surrounded me in my future workplace would be sharper, faster, and usually more intelligent than I would be. However, in rehabilitation I developed a new set of strengths. I prided myself on being able to see gaps and challenges in people and organizations, but more importantly, being able to see the strengths in others and bringing complementary skill sets together, creating a whole that is greater than the sum of the individuals. When faced with a problem, I facilitated a team of individuals with the unique skills that I could see they had, and the outcome would far surpass what one person could accomplish. This skill was the result of my own pursuit of self-awareness and learning to evaluate my own strengths and deficits during brain injury school—both equally important.

I put this skill to the test when Chris, my boss at the Ontario Fire Department, assigned me the task of building a new emergency operations center (EOC). An EOC is the environment where those with a role in managing a large incident converge. Historically, they are large empty spaces, such as a multi-use conference room or an extensive dedicated facility, that only gets used on the—thankfully—rare occasions when there's a major incident to resolve. The problem lies in their rare use; when non-emergency workers come to the facilities to deal with an incident, they feel uncomfortable because the facility is unfamiliar, cold, and unwelcoming.

In 2004, a hired consultant wrote a white paper detailing what that EOC in Ontario should entail. It was far too general and was based on building an over-the-top model that neglected many practicalities. Instead of following that guidance, I assembled representatives of the groups that would use the EOC in an emergency incident: city staff, community organizations, the Red Cross, local, state, and federal entities, utilities, hospitals, etc. I wanted to design and build an EOC that people would use for emergencies but also for other day-to-day activities in the city. Then, when faced with an emergency, they would be familiar with the space and ready to tackle the problem rather than waste time getting things up and running.

From an initial group of fifty representatives, I established a core team of fifteen people to help with the actual design, with strong representation from the IT department that was already known for their innovative approach to city challenges and facility improvements. We spent time dissecting the unique needs of the groups who would use the EOC. For example, most EOCs have one or two dispatch stations that are staffed only during a disaster, and typically the communications equipment in the EOC is outdated by the time it must serve its purpose. The assistant dispatch manager suggested building a new full-time dispatch center attached to the EOC, where the dispatchers wouldn't have to learn a new system when dealing with an emergency. We had conversations like that with every department and built one of California's most advanced, comprehensive, usable EOCs. Nearly every day the facility is used by departments for training classes and meetings. When it is activated to manage an incident, everyone feels at home, all equipment functions properly, and the uncertainty of operating in a foreign environment dissipates immediately.

People use the facility because they were involved in its creation. The team I put together enthusiastically got on board because I had an authentic desire for their input. I wanted the team to bring their best and show off their areas of expertise. My skill was identifying others' strengths and putting the team together. It was a skill that served me well in the workplace until it became a blind spot.

In 2016, I received a call from a colleague telling me about Ben Siegel, the new city manager in San Juan Capistrano. My colleague told me that Ben, thirty-six years old, was one of the youngest city managers in Orange County, but that he was sharp and had assembled an executive team from all across Southern California to rebuild a troubled organization. A large litigation profile, political instability, economic challenges, and a 25 percent workforce vacancy had given San Juan Capistrano an unfortunate reputation in the public sector profession. However, I got married in San Juan Capistrano; it was a special place to my family, and I certainly wasn't scared of diving into a bit of uncertainty at this point in my career. After one coffee with Ben, I knew he was exactly the type of person I wanted to work for, and this was a once-in-a-career opportunity to essentially reconstruct an organization in a community that I loved.

I made the transition from the City of Ontario, California, with 1,200 employees, to San Juan Capistrano, where the entire staff numbered eighty-two. In a small city with fewer human resources, each person wears multiple hats. In the beginning, I neglected the fact that my colleagues simply didn't have the bandwidth to participate on multiple teams. We were a smaller city with the same issues as a larger city, but fewer people to tackle those issues. I was often accused of holding too many meetings and bringing people together too often. My boss questioned why I included colleagues on a project rather than tackling it alone. And he was right. I had to be aware that if I assembled teams as I'd done in my previous job, I put an already limited workforce into a constrained environment.

I needed to shift my approach and figure out a better way, which meant modifying what I thought was my greatest strength. I had to become more independent and take more ownership of the issues, rather than delegate as I'd done in my past position. I used the people around me as sounding boards to occupy less of their time, yet still access their expertise. I saved the committee approach for only the highest of city priorities or the crisis of the quarter.

I had to see my blind spot and gain the self-awareness that the strength I had always valued was a crutch on which I could no longer depend. While I thought I was being inclusive and collaborative, I lacked awareness about the impact of my approach on my colleagues.

Working with a group of exceptional existing and new city staff under Ben's leadership and a cohesive and supportive city council, we have surpassed most of the goals set for the city. We have filled all vacancies and attracted new and financially-viable development into the community. We are building a reputation as an employer of choice, and our employees are designing and implementing a model workplace culture.

Part of building self-awareness is learning how to ask the right questions. New leaders must fight the desire to be the leader who has all the answers and strive to be the leader who has the ability to understand and gather all the right information and make the decisions that ultimately advance the mission of the organization instead. If you're a self-aware person, then you become good at listening, asking questions, and understanding another's perspective—which I'll talk about in chapter 2.

CHAPTER 2

IT'S LONELY AT THE TOP

A week before my first day on the job with the Ontario Police Department, the Police Chief invited me to a three-day strategic planning retreat in the mountains to discuss the future of the organization. I'd met some of my new colleagues already but not all of them. This sounded like a fantastic way to begin a new job: an off-site in the mountains to get to know everyone in a casual atmosphere, skip the awkward small talk around the water cooler, and quickly create bonds that would carry back to the workplace.

Instead, I felt like the new kid in the seventh-grade cafeteria. From the moment I parked my car in the conference center lot, I was flying solo. I attempted to make my way into one of the groups huddled in the parking lot, but I was ignored. As everyone went to put their bags in their cabins, I was left standing alone to figure out my room assignment. By process of elimination I found my assigned cabin, and I received the same awkward reception from my roommate. It was clear he felt he drew the short straw. I consoled myself with the thought that some people are shy and that the first group activity—a short hike around the lake—would be better.

Instead, I was at the very back of the pack, the gap between me and the rest of the team increasing with each step. With only myself to talk to, I imagined the thoughts going through their heads: "This guy's a civilian. We've never had a civilian on the police command staff. What's he doing here?" or "This guy comes from the fire department. They rescue kittens from trees and run around with hoses. What does he know about police work?"

When one of my fellow captains dropped back from the group, my mood brightened until he said, "Jacob, I just want to let you know," he said, pointing to the twenty or so people in front of me, "there's not a single person in that group that wants you here."

I thought, "Oh, joy. What a wonderful three days this will be; living, sleeping, breathing with my new friends here at the Ontario Police Department."

Clearly, my colleagues were not going to offer their total support for me in my new position, at least not initially. In every meeting over the next several months, one particular captain confronted and challenged me whenever I expressed an opinion. This captain repeatedly made it a point to show me that he was in charge, not the other way around.

In one of our initial leadership meetings, one of the tenured lieutenants raised his hand in the middle of the chief explaining a new area command concept and said, "Chief, I'm not so sure I'm comfortable talking about this topic. How do we know we can trust that guy?" as he pointed at me. Nobody responded, and the meeting ended shortly thereafter.

ESTABLISH TRUST, CALM YOUR ANXIETIES

We often think "If I were in charge, I would..." and fill in the blank with our ideas. When a promotion comes around, however, we find that leading a group and managing change is not as easy as we thought it would be. We also find that being the leader can be quite lonely.

Not all new leaders receive such blatant resistance when they join a new organization. Whether they are openly hostile or not, the existing team will have questions about the new leader's fitness for duty. They may not express their doubts, but they will all wonder why he got the position over them, or why he got the position over the person that they recommended, or what it is that he brings to the table. They wonder what he could possibly contribute that's new and fresh and exciting that they haven't already understood and tried within the organization.

When a new leader joins an existing team, some people will feel threatened and insecure. They may feel their direct line of authority is being questioned, and some colleagues may act in a way to undermine the credibility of the new leader.

What does a new leader do when no one wants him there? What happens when nobody will speak to him? What happens when he has to figure out where the bathroom is on his own? There are specific steps new supervisors and managers can take to reduce the resistance of the existing team and prove themselves worthy of respect and collaboration. By taking some time in the beginning of a new position to understand everyone's expectations and their unique needs and strengths, the new manager can build rapport with his new peers and team and identify the priorities that need to be addressed.

THE FIRST NINETY DAYS

Challenges with colleagues and the management team

may be apparent from day one. Regardless, leaders need to do their best to ascertain the quality of the working relationships from the onset. They must understand the expectations, concerns, fears, and needs of their colleagues and management team before moving forward with any new mandates or changes. By addressing the challenges from colleagues and the management team head on, the new leader eases his own insecurities and doubts that come with taking on a new position.

Michael D. Watkins, author of *The First 90 Days, Updated and Expanded: Proven Strategies for Getting Up to Speed Faster and Smarter,* has this to say:

> Aligning an organization is like preparing for a long sailing trip. First, you need to be clear on whether your destination (the mission and goals) and your route (the strategy) are the right ones. Then you can figure out which boat you need (the structure), how to outfit it (the processes), and which mix of crew members is best (the skill bases). Throughout the journey, you keep an eye out for reefs that are not on the charts.

When the rogue lieutenant questioned my presence and integrity at the management meeting, everyone remained silent. My office, however, was bustling in the twenty-four hours that followed. Several other lieutenants and captains came to my office to express their disdain for his ridicule and encouraged me to just keep moving forward. Most importantly, they complimented me for the way I responded by remaining professional and above board. This was my first inclination that I would be able to eventually merge with my sworn peers. I believe their willingness to share their thoughts with me was a direct result of my engagement with them from my first day; I showed genuine interest and respect for their jobs and not from a need to prove anything.

CONFIRMING THE BOSS'S EXPECTATIONS

When I began my position in the police department, my boss, the police chief, wanted me to come in and take care of business. He was the type of boss who shut his door and worked independently, and he wanted me to figure out my responsibilities. Within the first month of being in the position, I knocked on his door and asked for a little bit of his time, which he was willing to give. I had specific questions for him. His answers guided my initial actions in my new position.

The first step to reducing anxiety about a new position and a resistant peer group is understanding the boss's expectations. Managers are promoted or hired because they have excellent ways of doing business based on their previous position. If they immediately implement new ideas, new structures, efficiencies, models, and workflows, and the boss has a completely different set of expectations, they may wake up on Monday without a job. Many bosses will be upfront about their expectations, but if the boss is not a highly communicative type, new leaders may have to be proactive and ask more exploratory questions.

Asking the boss specific questions about his expectations will help the new manager gain insight as to how to succeed in the new position. Two questions in particular are helpful:

- What are his expectations?
- What are the top five things he wants to see happen in the next twelve months?

In addition to straightforward questions about expectations, asking questions about why he was hired can help him build self-awareness about the role and understand the strengths the boss sees in him, the reason he was put in the position. For example, he may think his strength is putting in new systems, while the boss may say, "No, I want you to be the clean-up person. I want you to be the person to fire the people that we've never been able to get rid of."

Armed with the answers to both sets of questions, the new manager can begin to figure out how to merge the boss's expectations and his own strengths.

A third set of questions about company culture and organizational landmines will also help the leader succeed. Choices made from a place of excitement and enthusiasm may go against ingrained company culture or remind everyone of someone they hated. Here are some questions to ask:

- What would get me fired tomorrow?
- What are the landmines that, if I'm excited and I go that route, will get me canned?
- How is this workplace unique from other environments in the company?
- What did the prior person who held my position do that alienated his peers, teams, or other stakeholders?

After working for four different departments in the city of Ontario over the course of eleven years, I took on my current position of assistant city manager of San Juan Capistrano. One of my first duties was to meet with the unions to learn about the culture and climate in the organization from their perspective. The city manager and I were planning to conduct quarterly all-hands meetings to gather everyone together and talk about key issues in the organization, and I presented this idea to the unions, asking if they thought it would be welcomed.

They agreed it was important but added, "Whatever you do, do not bring balloons." I composed myself before asking for an explanation. They explained that a predecessor brought balloons to an all-hands meeting and meant them as a sign of recognition and hard work. They added that if I were to show up with balloons, there would be a mutiny. This was extremely useful, albeit odd, information to have. Chances are I wouldn't have taken balloons to the all-hands meeting, but I might have brought them to a celebratory lunch and that would have been a mistake if done without their input. Leaders are well-served to identify these landmines and cultural challenges ahead of time with their boss, but it's even more important to get them reaffirmed from those they will be serving.

CREATE VALUE FOR PEERS

The mindset of the new leader must shift from one of commanding to one of serving. The new manager looks for ways to create the highest level of value for his colleagues by asking what they need that he could provide. The question is not, "what type of contribution and value can my colleague provide for me?" The new leader asks what he can contribute. In doing so, he begins to build trust and partnership with colleagues. There's one simple question that opens the dialogue between the new leader and colleagues and enables a positive rapport to be forged: **what is something you've always wanted that no one has been able to deliver?**

THE TOP FIVE

To start the conversation about expectations with my boss at San Juan Capistrano, I sent him an email a week before I started the position. I included a list of the thirty-seven qualities (see Appendix A) necessary to be an effective assistant city manager according to the International Association of City Managers (ICMA). I asked him to highlight his top five, which he did. He chose:

- Good/positive role model

- Trust and honesty

- Be able/willing to take on any project, task, or issue

- Excellent communication skills

- Influence without authority

We didn't know each other and had never worked together, but this exercise gave us a great opportunity to begin a discussion about expectations at a high level. It gave me more insight about the type of boss he was and the type of employee I needed to strive to become. From the onset, it showed me that we had shared values, and this was a catalyst for some additional questions that I could ask him to continue the conversation about expectations. For example, the last bullet, "Influence without authority" gave me the impression that I may not be directly over a number of employees on the organizational chart, and I would need to learn more about this structure before I dived in. Ben explained that many of the executives would report directly to him, and while he wanted me to be seen as an organizational leader with influence, I would have to do so in many situations without direct oversight of an employee or function. I was able to use this insight to develop strong relationships with my executive team colleagues and provide them with guidance without overstepping. An early misstep in this area could have cost me my ability to perform in lockstep with the team.

This process also allowed Ben to provide me with one of the best pieces of advice about job transition that I have received to date: "Use this opportunity to reinvent yourself." He explained that I should use this transition to think about ways to improve my approach and give myself a fresh lens through which to view my new surroundings.

Regularly checking in with the boss about their expectations to determine if they're still accurate and if expectations have changed is a good habit to form, but it's even better to understand his needs before your first day.

Brad Kaylor's fit physique and chiseled profile affectionately earned him the nickname "Calendar Brad" among his peers. The twenty-five-year SWAT team member was a forward-looking leader and all-around extraordinary person—witty, funny, charismatic—and my new colleague. Brad was a wonderful, likable person, universally respected by everyone in the department, sworn and civilian. On the other hand, I was a civilian coming from the outside who didn't have Brad's operational and tactical experience. While Brad was cordial to me, I don't believe he understood what I could add to the team until he was promoted to captain and I met with him to ask the following question: "Brad, what is something that you have always wanted to see here at the Ontario Police Department that nobody has ever been able to deliver for you?"

And Brad said, "Well, when we moved to this new Taj

Mahal of a building, we lost one of the former building's greatest assets: a shooting range. It used to be that when we got a new firearm or wanted to get in some extra practice, we just made our way to the basement and practiced qualifying. This new building opened without a range, and now we have to either use a dirty outdoor range at a public facility, or rent time at a smaller range at a neighboring police department outside of our service area. Now we have to leave our police department building, figure out our schedule coverage, and go somewhere else to shoot and qualify, sometimes without on-site access to our own experts."

The crux of the problem came forth, "It's demoralizing that a smaller police department has an indoor shooting range, and we, a large, model municipal police department, have to beg to use someone else's facility. If we are truly going to be a big city police department, if we're going to be self-sufficient, it would really be amazing for us to have our own police shooting range. We've always been told there's no money and no way."

I had only fired a firearm a couple times in my entire life. I didn't know the difference between a 9-millimeter and a .50-caliber weapon. I said, "Brad, would you mind if we went to lunch and you told me more about this issue?"

I knew that if I could deliver on something like a shooting

range or focus some of my energy and resources on Brad's needs, I could build his trust and partnership. By demonstrating that my presence was in alignment with his needs, his team's goals, and his vision for the organization, we could build a successful relationship. I also thought that if we built a relationship, this might go a long way in addressing one of the department's most disturbing and often repeated phrases: "If you aren't sworn, you aren't shit."

Watkins writes in *The First 90 Days*, "Leadership ultimately is about influence and leverage. You are, after all, only one person. To be successful, you need to mobilize the energy of many others in your organization." Following his advice, I pulled my fiscal services team together, grabbed my colleagues from Public Works and the Information Technology department, and we spent the next two years hustling and chasing every ounce of grant money we could find. We traveled throughout the United States and visited other agencies that had police shooting ranges. We interviewed contractors and consultants who built shooting ranges. We were bonded by our collective goal of achieving something that others dismissed, but so many craved. The team I created applied for and successfully received over two million dollars in grant money. We built an indoor training facility with a shooting range and state-of-the-art shoot house, giving the Ontario Police Department equipment that only a few other facilities in California had.

Reporters and public officials from all over the region came to the ribbon cutting to see the Ontario Police Department's new facility. It was a win for everyone in the organization. We saved money because our officers didn't have to drive to another shooting range, which meant they could shoot while on duty. The department increased training standards and began qualifying every month. My team and I established several partnerships as a result of focusing on the value I could provide. Other people came to our facility to train. And heck, they even let me do a little shooting—emphasis on "little."

A new leader doesn't have to build a two-million-dollar facility to bring value to the organization, but he does need to ask questions to demonstrate his willingness to serve. Ask questions like:

- What has never been done before here that you've always wanted to see?
- What would provide the greatest benefit to your team that's something that I could look into for you?
- What should I do each and every day to make your job easier?
- How can I provide value to you?

The underlying question of all of the questions is "how can I radically exceed your expectations?" I wasn't seeking information about Brad's day-to-day expectations or value that's easy to provide. I didn't want Brad to say, "Well, you can pay the bills for us every day." I wanted him to say, "You know what? For a decade, we've always wanted to have a shooting range here, and nobody has ever been able to find the money. A shooting range would be a game changer in the way we do business. But you know what, Jacob, it's totally impossible. Everybody who's attempted it has failed."

Providing extreme value moves the relationship from pedestrian to personal. The leader shows his peers and team that he's providing value beyond the simple expectations of the position, which others take for granted and aren't all that moved by.

Simply asking these questions solicits an initial response of respect. Just by going to your colleague and asking them how to be of service, shows a level of servant leadership. They drop their defenses. Instead of standing in the doorway, the new leader is invited in because everyone wants to feel like their needs are being met and that others care about what they need.

When I asked for Brad's insight, I was essentially saying, "What do you, Brad, feel that you need as the expert in this organization, and how could I possibly help you fill that gap, meet that need, and respond to your desires and interests?" This approach meets colleagues where they are instead of telling them what the answer is while creating a mutual partnership. He implies that in the future, when there are things that he or his team needs, he can turn to and lean on his colleagues.

UNDERSTANDING THE STAFF'S NEEDS

In the first ninety days, the new manager has accomplished two important information-gathering tasks: he has gained a clear understanding of the boss's expectations and insight as to how he can provide the highest level of value for his peers. As such, a support cycle is created: the new leader supports his peers and his peers support him, which helps him meet the boss's expectations and, more importantly, enables him to create and improve the atmosphere and environment for his staff.

In many of my positions, I was hired to be a change agent. I was brought in to fix an environment or help the team take their performance to the next level. In each case, before making any drastic changes or inserting ideals about how a perfect culture works, I spoke to the people who have spent time in the trenches—the staff. First, I held an all-hands meeting with everybody present. Everyone received the same message at the same time. At that all-hands meeting, the message usually had three parts:

1. I would set the tone: show optimism, respect, and

belief in the nobility of their position, and create a climate of collective responsibility for success.

2. I would decrease change anxiety: let the staff know that it will take time for them to see improvements. I reassured them that improvement is not going to be about massive overhaul. Improvement doesn't happen overnight and any changes that do occur will be small and incremental, not large and drastic.

3. Remember, no one responds well to catastrophic overnight change. The leader must minimize the staff's fear that they're going to come to work one morning and learn they have to wear a clown suit every day.

4. I would provide a roadmap for the next ninety days: I explained that I'd spend the first ninety days assessing the organization from different perspectives, including theirs, and that I would bring the group back together to share my findings.

I then conducted a series of one-on-one meetings, where I asked everyone the same eight to ten questions, like the following:

- What do you feel are the greatest strengths of this current operation?
- What are the biggest challenges faced by this current operation?
- What is one environmental change that you would like to see occur in this operation?

- Are you satisfied where you are?
- Do you want to grow and develop?
- If so, how do you want to see yourself grow and develop?
- What are three professional development goals that you have for yourself?
- What warnings and advice do you have for me in this operation?
- What are the landmines that you don't want to see me step on?
- What's the first change you believe I should consider?
- What do you want to ensure doesn't change in our workplace?
- What questions do you have for me?

It's important to ask everyone the same questions, which provides a baseline and an understanding of the state of the organization and the culture. These questions demonstrate my investment in the staff's success, which in turn helps them invest in the new leadership.

At the end of the one-on-one meeting, I ask the person to sign an expectations memo. It reads:

> *Thank you so much for meeting with me today. I'm going to use the information in our discussion to create a plan that I will deliver to the organization after ninety days. It's going to be the roadmap for our next chapter. In the meantime, please adhere to the following three expectations:*

1. Service: all employees are expected to maintain a high level of customer service for internal and external clients. Phone etiquette and follow-through must be executed. We must keep in mind our role as public servants and our unique position as the first (and sometimes only) point of contact with our clientele.

2. Professional Development: professional development shall be encouraged and supported. Budget constraints may require employees to consider creative training options and/or the development of in-house training programs.

3. Catch People Doing Things Right: please notify your supervisor if you see a colleague demonstrating exceptional skills and/or customer service.

Thank you so much for sharing all of your ideas with me today. I will use these ideas to formulate the transition and the strategic plan for our organization. Please understand this was a brainstorming session only. I will not be able to incorporate all of your ideas for change. You will not see all of your ideas for change incorporated into our roadmap. There will be restrictions, both legally and financially, that will prohibit your good ideas from being a part of my change and transition plan.

I ask that you continue to bring all of your suggestions to me, so I can make that determination. Please do not limit yourself in what you share with me in the future. Thank you so much for your honesty.

This is your copy of the memo. I am issuing this memo to all of your peers after their one-on-one sessions.

This process decreases the staff's anxieties. It gives them the understanding that I am committed to understanding their perspective, yet still sets realistic expectations. They can't be disappointed when they don't see the new paint on the wall even though they told you it's everybody's top priority.

New leaders sometimes think they have all the answers—they must, they were hired to do the job. Assumptions are a dangerous thing to have. Quoting Watkins again from *The First 90 Days,* "Transition failures happen because new leaders either misunderstand the essential demands of the situation or lack the skill and flexibility to adapt to them." Unless leaders ask the right questions and gain a 360-degree view of the new environment, they can't begin to truly move forward and help themselves or others to be successful. This process of really engaging and exploring the boss, peers, and staff is the only way for the new leader to make sure that he'll be able to add value.

LET YOUR WORK SPEAK FOR ITSELF

Chris Hughes joined the fire service after high school and a short stint as a bartender, ultimately working his way up through the ranks to fire chief. He was a political shark and a leadership guru, and I wanted to crack the leadership code by emulating him.

After working in the fire department as the disaster preparedness analyst for ten months, I was promoted to emergency manager, which meant I officially had three roles: emergency manager, grant writer, and public information officer. I went to my first fire as the public information officer in early 2006, and wrote a press release when I returned to the station. I wrote,

> *"At 2:25 p.m., the City of Ontario received a 911 call reporting smoke and fire coming from a large commercial recycling facility. The first engine company on scene confirmed heavy smoke and fire and a second alarm was dispatched to the fire. The combustibles on scene burned for over six hours and the damage was contained to the recycling facility. According to Fire Chief Chris Hughes, 'We train daily for this type of large incident and the extraordinary actions of our firefighters contained the fire to one facility and prevented the neighborhood from becoming an inferno.'"*

Chris crossed out the last sentence and said, "Let's just let our work speak for itself." He was the only executive I knew in the public safety realm who said, "no more quotes from the fire chief." From that day on, I never quoted Chris in another fire press release because he wanted to make sure that our work spoke for itself and the credit went to others, not to those in a leader-ship capacity.

On another occasion, I said to Chris, "Now that I've been promoted to emergency manager in the fire department and received my graduate degree, how should I frame my email signature? How many degrees should I put in my email signature?" And he said, "Jacob, just let your work speak for itself." For as long as I worked for him, he never once took credit for anything that he did and never once told a war story, yet he commanded and deserved respect from the entire fire department and the rest of the city. It was no wonder he later became the chief executive—City Manager of Ontario.

When leaders feel insecure and that they have a lot to prove, their instinct is to tell colleagues about their past successes in an effort to demonstrate their worthiness of the new position. I have been guilty of this many times in my career. Letting the work speak for itself is more powerful. Leaders establish themselves as experts by doing the work and showing the value they bring to the organization.

TRANSITION PERIOD

When I left the police department in Ontario, I was over-seeing a staff of seventy. I went from a career in public safety, to a department head role in city hall when I was promoted to business operations director of Ontario's Economic Development Agency with a five-person staff. I was responsible for business attraction, business retention, workforce development, marketing, communications, and supported the staff overseeing land deal negotiations and real property management. I had no experience in economic development. Zero. The five employees I supervised knew far more than I did. They knew it and I knew it, and all of a sudden, I was going to be their boss. They might have heard my name previously but certainly had no understanding of my previous city roles.

I understand now that the city manager had promoted me for my ability to lead, create partnerships, and build a strong team. Despite his confidence in me, I felt lost and terrified on the first day. When I extended my handshake to one of my direct reports on the first day, he said, "How did you get here?" This was my employee! In public safety, he would have been sent home for insubordination or hung on the flag pole by his boxers, but now I was outside of public safety. Things were a little bit different, and he felt empowered to make a demeaning comment.

In my new role I had the good fortune of reporting to the Economic Development Director, John Andrews. John was a veteran public servant, having played a major role in rebuilding the city of Riverside and the city of Pasadena before making his way to Ontario a few years later. As an attendee in a city leadership program, I'd heard John speak two years earlier and left his speech fascinated by economic development, but even more impressed with John. He conveyed authentic enthusiasm for his job and the city. I left his training seminar thinking that working for him someday would be an amazing opportunity to grow in a completely new area. And there I was. John cared deeply about the professional development of other employees and was totally invested in the team's growth. Although I'd been placed in the role by the city manager, he didn't show any animosity. In fact, in our first meeting he said, "Jacob, I want you to attend all of my meetings with me. We have one today with a local developer on a major project in about an hour. I want you to spend some time getting immersed and listening in on the conversations and the negotiations that we partake in here in economic development." He didn't give me any projects or programs. He gave me insight on the interpersonal dynamics of some of my new employees, but mostly he gave me permission just to tag along, even though I felt like a fourth grader battling once again with imposter syndrome.

John had strong city manager mentors in the business, and he was always looking to return the favor. My team benefited from his commitment to others.

In most new positions, leaders feel they have to make immediate decisions. They want to change, do, and manage things. They want to lead. John Andrews felt I should follow before I could lead.

The transition period gave me an opportunity to be an observer. I spent several weeks attending meetings with him and meeting different people, until the training wheels could slowly come off. The gradual momentum allowed me to shake more hands, visit key properties, and represent the city at community events and meetings. I began to see the gaps, especially those where I could add value. The gaps I saw were not in property negotiations or real estate development. John and my colleague Charity had that nailed. The gaps were in marketing, advertising, and communications. The previous City Manager, Greg Devereaux, had built a city as a corporate entity, one responsible to stakeholders, and one that associated business investment with community prosperity. As a result, Ontario thrived and became, and still is, one of the strongest municipal organizations in the state, perhaps the country. But there was room to take this corporate philosophy to the next level by polishing the brand and focusing on outreach. I grabbed at the opportunity to use my media relations background to contribute to building the brand of the city, which would support my boss's ability to encourage developers to invest.

If I had tried to understand the entire department on day

one and focused on real estate and land development, I would have missed seeing the opportunities where I could provide value. In a relatively short time, I was seen as someone who had a knack for municipal brand development, communications, and marketing. Ultimately, I was promoted to my next position because of that success. I credit most of my success to John. He encouraged his team members to contribute and to bring their differences and diversity to the table. He was an inclusive leader who wanted to make sure that everyone had the opportunity to fill the gaps they were best equipped to fill.

John was a wonderful teacher who allowed me to learn, observe, and diagnose on my own. He let me control the hiring process, which allowed me to onboard total rock stars who have continued to move up in the city, one of whom I even stole later to hire as my assistant.

When the new leader takes the observer role and transitions more slowly to the new position, he can see clearly what's taking place and start to identify the gaps where he can add value.

SMOOTH TRANSITIONS

I never forgot how smooth John Andrews made the transition to the Economic Development Agency for me.

Later in my career, when my colleague David was promoted from a city clerical position to an analyst position reporting to me, I wanted him to have a similar experience. We met briefly on his first day, and I said, "We're not going to meet for a few weeks. I want you to get your office set up into a comfortable environment. I want you to tell me what tools and resources you need to make your office the most functional. I want you to get your bearings by reading as much as you can from your predecessor and "interviewing" our city's subject matter experts. I want you to start to look at training classes that you might be interested in. I don't want you to start tackling projects right now. I want to keep the Inbox as empty as I can for you."

He picked up a lamp, a few paintings, and some comfortable furniture at a garage sale. (I would have approved those purchases, but that gives you a glimpse into how seriously he takes his public servant role.) He started to make himself at home. When a new employee is given the opportunity to transition, their chances for success increase. I said to David, "Let me know when you feel settled and then we can meet and create your work plan and start thinking about where we're going with the projects and priorities of the organization. A couple weeks isn't going to hurt anybody, and the organization's going to continue just fine."

The quality of work a calm employee brings greatly outweighs the cost of waiting a few weeks to give the new employee space to settle in. David approached me when he was ready to talk. Having all of his tools and resources in place made a positive impact for him. It allowed him to approach my needs and my priorities with a clear idea of where the organization was, and having his own systems in place was a confidence booster. So many times, a boss will meet with a new employee on day one and say, "This is your deadline on this. This is what I need you to do for this. This is who I need you to meet with. This is who I need you to talk to," without giving the new employee an opportunity to breathe, get their systems and structures in place, move into their environment, and then come ready to go.

Every time I've tried to get an employee moving too quickly in their promotion, I've witnessed shutdown. It's an ineffective way to onboard a new employee. The more time and opportunity to settle, decrease the stimulation, return to the midline, and put compensatory techniques in place that work, the more prepared and effective the employee will be to tackle the projects, programs, and priorities.

CHAPTER 3

MIND THE GAP

When you're in city government and you want to study the best of the best, a good place to start is the SWAT team. With its highly trained officers and state-of-the-art equipment, Ontario SWAT was a model in Southern California that was often called upon to support other agencies in critical incidents.

When I was Ontario's emergency manager, I was tasked with building a new mobile command vehicle for joint use by the fire and police departments. The city's existing command vehicle resembled the 1921 Oldsmobile Model 43-A touring car used by the Beverly Hillbillies. Called the "Bookmobile," it had been donated to public safety from the city library decades prior, and no public safety professional dared to be caught inside of it, both for safety reasons and fear of public humiliation! When I was first hired at the fire department, we secured state and federal funding to design and build a new forty-two-foot command vehicle. During that time, I worked with SWAT leadership to make sure the vehicle's design would meet their needs. After completion, I'd roll out with the vehicle to set it up and make sure the communications and IT systems functioned properly.

When I transitioned to the police department and found myself in the same department as SWAT, I wanted to take the opportunity to study them and learn how I could take my civilian divisions up to that elite level. I asked the SWAT commander if I could start going out more regularly with the team to observe their activities. I was more interested in their team dynamics and leadership expertise and less concerned about the new vehicle's functionality. I explained that I'd be able to do my job better if I had a better understanding of SWAT operations. His response—remember, these were the people who didn't want me on their camping retreat—was, "Okay, fine, whatever." I asked dispatch to page me on all of the SWAT calls no matter the time of day or night. When the page came at 1 a.m., I deployed with the SWAT team. I drove my personal vehicle, a dated Toyota Tacoma pickup truck, into unique neighborhoods, pulled up to the given address, and watched the SWAT team in action. I watched call after call after call, usually positioned a few feet from the SWAT commander.

Contrary to the popular depiction of tanks breaking down

walls and detonating bombs within minutes of arriving on scene, SWAT operations are usually slow—painfully slow (unless there is an imminent threat to someone inside of a structure, but that is rare; in most cases, the suspect is barricaded inside on his own). The deployments are long and calculated. Seldom, if ever, does the SWAT team have to make a dynamic entry and rescue the three innocent children from a drug-dealing kidnapper.

On a typical operation, everyone arrives on the scene, a strong perimeter is established, and teams deploy to various positions, both adjacent to the structure and from strategic locations. From the command post, the SWAT commander radios instructions to the team. I would hear commands like, "Zulu 8 move twenty feet to the west; Zulu 29 advance ten feet forward toward the structure and hold." The SWAT commander huddles over a map with his leadership team and moves people around to gather intelligence. The more information he can gather, the more accurate his situational awareness will be. His ultimate goal is to decrease risk and increase the safety of the personnel and the people involved in the operation. When no immediate threat is present to innocent parties, SWAT calls can last many hours; the longest I was ever on scene was fourteen hours. The SWAT commander tries every strategy and tactic in the book before resorting to a dynamic, explosive entry.

I had the privilege to sit with the SWAT commander, the hostage negotiators, and the bomb robot technicians. I studied every member of the team in their environment. After many call outs, I noticed that officers who were on the scene for four or five hours in the Southern California heat drank a lot of water, which meant they had to eventually...urinate—as did all the support personnel on-scene. When a SWAT team member had to pee, he had to call the SWAT commander, who had to find a replacement for him. The replacement went to the position of the member who needed relief. The replacement had to be briefed, then the officer who had to pee left his position and found a police car and drove to the local twenty-four-hour gas station. Then, the process went in reverse: returning to the scene, getting briefed, and returning to the position. In many cases, when there wasn't a surplus of officers readily available to cover for the SWAT officer, the local tree might become the closest relief area, which sometimes created other PR and safety issues.

I noticed the time and personnel resources needed to allow the SWAT officers to pee. I started thinking, "What if, instead of the SWAT team going to the bathroom, the bathrooms came to them? How could we fix this problem and create more efficiency in this process?" A few SWAT call outs later, I asked the SWAT commander if I could deploy toilets to the scene. He looked at me with a puzzled face, suspecting that I was highly intoxicated and asked, "What are you talking about?" I repeated my request, and much like when I'd first asked if I could deploy on SWAT calls, he said, "Whatever, whatever, just do your thing."

Between the time I first had the idea, and the SWAT call out when I made my request, I had created a spreadsheet where I'd collected information about every Porta-Potty in Southern California. I knew the cost. I knew the size. I knew the type of toilet paper that was deployed with it. I knew the hand wash stations that were available. I knew which ones were deadly and which were suitable for the Grammys. I knew the name of every manager of every Porta-Potty shop. I knew the response time. I opened the binder and called one of the contracts I had put together, and within thirty minutes I had eight Porta-Pottys deployed around the SWAT scene. This time when the officer had to call in and use the bathroom, the SWAT commander was able to say, "No problem. There's a honey bucket twenty-five feet away." This radically cut down on the time an officer left his position and resolved the real efficiency gap that I had seen.

I had no SWAT training. I knew nothing about tactics, or take downs, or dynamic entries, but I could see a gap that existed. I was able to draw on my experience of managing contracts and logistics and see a way that I could add value. Overnight, the SWAT operations eliminated waste and took things up a notch. The SWAT team was blown away—pardon the pun—that there were Porta-Pottys on scene. To me, it wasn't that big of a deal, but to them, it was more about someone looking out for their interests, no matter how small, when they were putting everything on the line for others.

I started thinking about what else I could do; were there other support gaps where I could help the SWAT team focus on their mission and take this already elite SWAT team to the next level? I formed the Tactical Information Technology team, affectionately known as the TIT team—not the most thought out acronym, but it worked.

The group comprised eight civilian IT and public works employees. We deployed with the SWAT team to provide secondary support, such as bringing food to the scene rather than sending the SWAT officers out for meals. We tested all different types of technologies based on our understanding of their needs and gaps: testing cameras and tablets on tripods throughout the area of the scene to send information back to the command post, testing new wireless networks, and supporting the acquisition and implementation of lots of new technology. To this day, a support team deploys on most SWAT calls (though I believe they've changed the name). The support team members are not police officers. Their mission is to support the SWAT team and fill the gaps that only someone with a radically different perspective and background can identify.

Leaders can implement a similar technique by reaching out to parallel departments. For example, when a major company initiative is being planned and the standard team comprises marketing, sales, and operations, a couple representatives from IT could be asked to join. The initiative may have nothing to do with technology, but the IT folks bring a different perspective to the project. While the standard team looks at the challenge from the perspective of customer behavior and product feasibility and conducts surveys to gather data, A GIS specialist might put together impressive maps that show the demographic data conveyed by the survey. A whole new level of "wow" is created when the initiative is presented to the executive team. A software development guru might be able to offer up some insight as to how improvement and modification of the company's current app could attract new customers by incorporating a few new features that are available on the app market. Their input comes from a place of little to no marketing, sales, and operations expertise, but might just help broaden the success of the new initiative and prevent the project from looking like every other company roll out. Dave Hager, President and CEO of Devon Energy Corporation, a company with a $12.2 billion market cap, sums it up best: "Without unique backgrounds and viewpoints, you can't do business differently. We take that notion to heart in everything we're doing to enhance our operations."

CRISIS OR PROBLEM

After successfully achieving the EMT certification and engaging in various EMT volunteer roles, I decided to pursue a career as a police dispatcher. Now at the tail end of brain school, I applied all my new skills to a certification course and state exam, this time passing all the tests without much difficulty. My good fortune continued as I was hired part-time at a local department and later in a full-time capacity; finally, I was able to start paying off some of my bills and achieve a certain level of independence.

One of the most important lessons I learned early on as a dispatcher was that there are few crises and everything else is just a problem to be solved. The classification depends on the point of view.

Dispatchers receive 911 calls all day long. Some calls are people who have simply reached their breaking point, like the person who screams and yells that they have an emergency, demanding a police officer come to the scene. They're upset because their neighbor's parked car is sticking into their driveway. They are convinced that this is an emergency and a police officer needs to get there immediately, because they've been dealing with this problem for a year. Other calls are life or death situations, such as the elderly person who falls down a flight of stairs and has a bleeding head wound, or the fire that's trapped a family in a third-story apartment.

The dispatcher has the responsibility to prioritize that call in the computer-aided dispatch system. It may be the biggest crisis the caller has ever faced, but the dispatcher has to decide if it's a number one priority, a number ten priority, or somewhere in between.

Police officers, fire fighters, and EMS professionals understand life and death because they see it every day. They don't tend to see everything as a crisis. They tend to see everything as a situation to solve with their training and skills. Outside of public safety, it can seem that every problem is a crisis. People scream and yell and get worked up over things that are just problems to be solved, not crises.

The leader has to step back from the noise and ask, "Is this an emergency where I need to drop everything and make sure everyone understands the significance, or is it just something that needs to be solved? Can I methodically and strategically apply the appropriate people and resources, and get the problem addressed in its appropriate time, and place, and prioritization, like a SWAT team?"

Many leaders want to be in charge of everything in the workplace. They want to feel like they're doing a great job. They want to be invincible, invulnerable, and problem-free. Anyone who works in an organization knows that "problem-free" is not reality. Because of pressure in the workplace, new leaders may interpret the sense of being out of control as a crisis. The emotional instability of a leader who treats everything as a crisis will burn people out. New leaders need to create an environment where people understand that they can be comfortable with problems that need to be solved and that few things are a crisis.

Part of identifying the gaps or problems is also making sure that the team stays on a stable ship that's focused on the mission of the organization and not constantly derailed by the boss's insecurity, fears, and neurosis in making everything an emergency when it rarely is.

ORGANIZING A CRISIS

One of the first things I do when faced with a major challenge at work is create an organizational chart. I've gotten used to my colleagues poking fun at me about this obsession. Within a few minutes of a meeting, someone will say, "I know Jacob is already working on the org chart," which is true.

I love org charts for many reasons. One of which is that

my injury enhanced my visual memory after the auditory learning and processing center of my brain sustained some damage. This has worked to my advantage. To identify gaps, I visually think about how to put an overwhelming crisis or challenge into boxes, literally. I then create teams and identify people on the teams and the responsibilities they'll take on. Almost without exception, within an hour of starting the meeting on a new project, there's an org chart. Even if it was the butt of a joke an hour earlier, the org chart creates a level of comfort for everyone because what seem to be overwhelming tasks can be accomplished, and most people thrive in clear accountability (contrary to some modern management theorists that laud blurred accountability).

I learned about this method when I began working as an emergency manager. In the 1970s, the fire service in California developed the Incident Command System (ICS) in which every incident, no matter how large or small, could be represented with a clear chain of command and a manageable span of control on an org chart. I use the same system to create order out of change and chaos.

My reputation as the "org chart guy" was well known. When I was a low-level emergency manager in Ontario, I was called to City Manager Greg Devereaux's office—yes, that same Greg Devereaux who three years later would convince me to transfer to the police department by quoting Shakespeare. Being summoned to the city manager's office was not the norm at my level in the organization. My boss, yes, but not me. I knew this was something significant. As I approached his office, Greg met me in the hallway and said, "Jacob, we're going to go into my conference room. Follow my lead." I swallowed and said, "Okay."

Greg was respected both inside and outside the organization and when he gave direction, everyone followed without hesitation. The sixty or so people in the room came to attention when we entered. He said, "Everybody, this is Jacob. He's our city's emergency manager. Jacob, this is everybody." He continued, "Effective immediately, I am making the issue of homelessness a city disaster." He'd made homelessness an emergency management project and put me in charge of a topic I knew nothing about. He said he would return to the conference room in two hours, and our mission was to create a comprehensive org chart representing the sixty or so people in the room and an appropriate approach to the problem.

He left the room, and I saw sixty faces blinking and staring at me in total silence. We began with introductions, and I facilitated a conversation about why this group of people had been gathered to confront the issue of homelessness. The homeless population of Ontario was growing rapidly; a "tent city" was growing in open land adjacent to the airport. Outside groups were threatening a lawsuit against the city of Ontario for allegedly targeting the homeless population. A perceived lack of resources for the homeless left them with few options except the occupation of city bus stops and vacant parcels. My job was to help create order out of chaos, to put in systems and strategies that would calm a situation that was rapidly spiraling out of control.

After introductions and asking a few questions to obtain some context, I decided to give an ICS 101 class, as there were many attorneys, non-profit agencies, and other non-city folks in the room that had never heard of emergency management. I drew five boxes on the dry erase board and begin filling in names and branches based on what the people in the room said were the goals of a homeless operation.

Greg returned to the conference room two hours later, and we successfully presented our org chart and initial plan. The room was packed full of experts, so it wasn't my role to come up with the best approach; rather, it was my job to facilitate, quarterback, and put everyone on the same page moving forward under a clear set of goals. I continue to lead in that manner to this day.

That meeting led to an intensive seven-day operation during which we addressed the issue of homelessness based on the org chart and an incident action plan that the team created. The model we developed was wildly successful and went on to be emulated by other cities.

ICS org charts are not your typical who-reports-to-whom hierarchies. In the homeless situation, the primary incident director at the top of the org chart was actually a mid-level manager who was outranked by many of the senior leadership in the room, but he was the subject matter expert. The deputy city manager, one of the highest positions in the city, had a finance position box in the homeless org chart based on his mastery of financial management and purchasing principles, which would be very important during this operation. The org chart is always based on matching people's talents and strengths with their appropriate place based on the type of incident, regardless of their tenure and their day-to-day position in the organization.

ICS org charts are a way of visually taking a crisis down a notch or two, until it's considered a problem to be solved. I've applied this technique to hundreds of issues, challenges, and projects in my tenure. Everyone may joke about me being the org chart guy, but at the end of the day, everyone benefits from it.

The org chart is literally a way of getting everybody on the same page. It's the starting point of creating calm in a crisis. All the players understand their role and responsibilities, what they're accountable for, and where they fit. The org chart communicates a clear reporting structure with an achievable span of control.

There may be resistance and consternation until the management process unfolds. But it works so effectively it doesn't take long for people to see that an ICS org chart is needed to tackle challenging, crisis-level issues, and it can be helpful for just about any project or problem, regardless of whether or not life and property are at stake!

SETTING PRIORITIES

Leaders have an obligation to advance the mission of the organization. Their goal is not to make others happy, but to enhance performance. They identify problems or gaps by asking the questions and accepting feedback about the weaknesses and challenges in the organization (as described in the previous chapter). With that information, they can then prioritize the issues and problems, thereby avoiding making rash decisions that don't specifically address the problems in the organization.

If a leader tries to take on all of the problems at once, she will fail. Her resources will be spread too thin, and her people won't be able to celebrate any victory, because too many open-ended and unsolved problems will have surfaced. She'll have talked about everybody's dirty laundry without bringing detergent to the party.

The examination, announcement, and conveyance of priorities to the team is just as important as identifying the problems. The leader is responsible for establishing where time and energy will be focused. Priorities must be achievable. In brain-injury rehabilitation, we set goals that are achievable. Each goal is a baby step toward the next, bigger goal. A leader, too, rolls out goals that can be achieved. She lets the team know immediately which items cannot be addressed due to legal, financial, or other reasons. Employees want to receive information in its entirety from the leader, not piecemeal and not from a game of "Telephone."

When the leader sets goals that are grandiose and unachievable, the staff feels frustrated. At the end of the year they say, "The self-assessment process was a total waste of time, because the situation is the same today as it was a year ago." In announcing priorities, the new leader takes ownership in figuring out what can be achieved and how people can jump on board.

As assistant city manager of San Juan Capistrano, I handle irate callers or those who feel dissatisfied with our service. For example, a resident may call and tell me that they called Code Enforcement to report election signs illegally posted in a park and haven't received a response. I never apologize off the bat, because I'm only receiving one side of the story. I finish the call, contact my staff, and ninety-nine percent of the time, there is a reasonable explanation for the service delay. When there isn't, I apologize and do my best to mitigate the issue. Often, an irate resident will call about a policy issue that is not under the purview of the city, such as problems with local schools. Schools have their own structure and their own elected officials that sit on a school board. I'll explain the limitations of our authority, and sometimes I have to be direct and say, "There is nothing further we can do regarding your concern; here are some options for you to consider." In general, residents are usually satisfied, even when the answer is "no," as long as the answer is direct and they are not given the runaround. As the leader, I set the priorities for our team and I do my best to communicate those priorities directly to the team and, in some cases, to the public. Prioritization and direct communication of those priorities is the leader's responsibility.

EMBRACING COGNITIVE DIVERSITY

A few years ago, I learned about the important work being done by Human Insight and their internationally-utilized AEM-Cube Assessment. Since then, I have been sharing it with all my audiences.

The AEM-Cube gives leaders insight about the contributions that may be missing from their team, division, or area of responsibility. It helps leaders see the functional blind spots that hold a team back from excellence. It reveals a team's strengths, weaknesses, and opportunities for improvement. Before leaders begin to look at the people around them, however, they need to look at themselves, and the AEM-Cube allows leaders that critical insight. Well over a thousand companies throughout the world have been using the AEM-Cube to build stronger teams that can best face change and future growth.

AEM stands for Attachment, Exploration, and Managing contribution. The assessment was developed by Peter Robertson based on concepts developed in the late 1980s, with the actual AEM-Cube instrument itself finalized and validated throughout the 1990s and 2000s.

Years later, Alison Reynolds and David Lewis conducted research over a two-year period based on these concepts and Peter Robertson's work. Reynolds and Lewis presented teams with a series of challenges and timed how fast they could solve the challenges. They determined that teams with higher levels of cognitive diversity are more successful in facing change and challenge in the workplace than homogeneous teams. The results were published in the *Harvard Business Review* (March 2017) in their article titled, "Teams Solve Problems Faster When They're More Cognitively Diverse."[1]

Diversity has become a buzzword in many fields, and no doubt people from different ethnicities, sexual orientations, or abilities bring different perspectives and experiences to the workplace. However, cognitive diversity goes deeper and transcends the physical differences used to define diversity. According to their research, cognitive diversity is comprised of two components:

- **Knowledge processing**: does the individual as a team member utilize only existing knowledge, or does she generate new knowledge in new situations?

- **Expertise perspective**: does she have a broader perspective of expertise and recognize the perspective that comes from others, in addition to what she brings to the table?

Reynolds and Lewis found that the teams with the highest levels of cognitive diversity, who embraced external knowledge and expertise, and had members who offer different paradigms solved problems the fastest. To create teams that are able to face change and to solve major challenges, leaders must recruit and develop teams that are cognitively diverse. They can really only make this a reality by using a tool like the AEM-Cube to evaluate strengths, challenges, and opportunities. There are four key benefits to building cognitively diverse teams:

1. *Cognitive diversity can generate accelerated results*. Many managers lead successful teams and want to take them to the next level. For example, the dispatch center may be processing 911 calls without difficulty. They're saving lives and putting out fires, but I want to take them to the next level to see if they can improve their performance, call processing time, and feel more fulfilled and connected to the mission. Leaders who want to make a good environment great may find cognitive diversity and the AEM-Cube helpful to accelerate results. Cognitive diversity integrates the contribution of people with the delivery of services and/or products to clients, together defined as the strategic diversity in teams. For example, if teams lack members contributing to the first stage of the growth-curve, there is an innovation gap.

If there are no team members in the middle stages of the growth-curve, there is an execution gap. If there are no team members contributing to the later stages of the growth-curve, compliance, quality, and efficiency are missing. Cognitive diversity is the key component in integrating and connecting these different contributions into an optimally-functioning system.

2. *Like-minded teams are the norm.* Leaders tend to form teams without cognitive diversity. When recruiting, leaders tend to form teams of like-minded individuals who are susceptible to groupthink and who have the same perspective. Those types of teams are the lowest performing in the study. The study says the teams that perform the best are those with a greater level of cognitive diversity. Leaders have to fight this natural tendency to bring people together from the same perspective. It's our natural tendency to stay with our tribe, but that actually creates an impediment to ultimate achievement in the workplace.

3. *Recruit for cognitive diversity and strategic diversity.* When the leader has properly assessed their team, maybe with the AEM-Cube assessment, they begin to see the gaps. They then have to figure out how to work with human resources or how to create a greater level of cognitive diversity. The interview process may need to be modified to identify candidates who will bring the cognitive diversity that fills the identified gap.

4. *Cognitive diversity is hard to see.* Research shows that when a group of executives is told "Raise your hand if you think you're a diverse bunch of people," everybody will raise their hand and say, "Oh yeah, we're really diverse." The research concluded that most teams, despite the perception of leadership, are not actually cognitively diverse. It's not enough to simply look at a team of people and say, "Yeah, they look diverse"; a tool is needed to properly evaluate.

The AEM-Cube has been successfully used by companies from healthcare to retail, from high-tech startups to nuclear facilities to identify an organization's strategic and cognitive diversity for performance optimization. The outcome of going through an AEM-cube assessment process is the ability for leadership to create teams that can interact effectively and ensure the greatest contribution from each individual, team, and unit for maximum productivity and profit.

WHEN A GAP CAN BE A BRIDGE

The leader's responsibility includes evaluating and assessing the gaps in process as well as the gaps in the people. While process gaps are problems to be solved, people gaps are weaknesses that are balanced by strengths. No one person has only strengths and no one person only has weaknesses; it is diversity among the people that takes a team or organization to the next level.

Each of us brings a series of strengths and challenges to the table. Just like each team has a series of strengths and gaps, so does every organization.

New managers want to depend on that which made them successful up to the point of their promotion. The newly promoted manager should pause and remember that all she depended upon previously was great in the previous

---

1 Alison Reynolds and David Lewis, "Teams Solve Problems Faster When They're More Cognitively Diverse," Harvard Business Review (March 2017). https://hbr.org/2017/03/teams-solve-problems-faster-when-theyre-more-cognitively-diverse?autocomplete=true

role. The new role will bring a new set of challenges and a new set of insecurities, inefficiencies, and gaps which will likely need a new set of tools—tools that she may not have used before. Instead of zooming into the new position and applying all those things that made her successful before, she should take a minute to think about what tools and techniques she'll need to be successful in the new endeavor. She should also consider looking at the new environment through the eyes of her new team and not be limited by her own paradigm.

In brain injury rehabilitation, I learned early on that the event that happened to me, the attack in the Berkeley BART Station, was the crisis. Everything that followed could be methodically figured out by bringing the right people together, leaning heavily on others, and approaching it in a strategic and well-thought-out way. Rather than scream and yell, take a deep breath, assess the problem, and then develop strategies and techniques to compensate for it.

CHAPTER 4

———

BUILD COMPENSATORY TECHNIQUES

One of the most debilitating residual effects of my brain injury is light sensitivity. Within just a few minutes of being exposed to fluorescent light, a dull throbbing begins in my left temple with a sharp pain behind my left eye that quickly escalates to a pounding migraine. The only solution is to retreat to a dark room until the pain stops, often twenty-four hours after it began—only to re-enter the world of fluorescent light and risk starting the cycle again.

Unfortunately for me, government buildings are obsessed with fluorescent light; nothing says bureaucracy like the cold pale glare and flicker of a fluorescent light bulb—and let's not forget just about every doctor's office, ER, hospital, and most retail stores. When I first began working in a fluorescent-lit government environment, my success on a daily basis was limited. I missed many days of work, but I didn't quit after my first fluorescent-light-induced migraine, nor did I resign to my condition and say, "Well, this is something that I have to deal with." I applied the lessons I'd learned in rehabilitation and pursued a series of compensatory techniques.

When I was first hired by the city of Fountain Valley as the part-time assistant to the emergency services coordinator early in my career, I was assigned a cubicle. Cubicles are open spaces, unprotected from the elements. That wasn't going to suffice, but I certainly wasn't going to ask for an office and be laughed out of the building on my first week in the job. My wife and I went to the office on a Sunday, armed with cardboard boxes, scissors, and duct tape, and built cubicle walls and a partial ceiling to block the light and allow for installation of my projector, which would take the LCD computer monitor image (fluorescent backlit display—pre-LED years) and provide the darker lighting conditions I needed to do my work. It looked a lot less like a fort than it sounds. It was inventive, understated, and would get the job done. I came in on Monday morning and a huge sea of staff had assembled around my cubicle. "What is this???????" everyone seemed to say at the same time. I just smiled and said I had some visual issues, and this would be a cheap solution. I'm not sure if they respected the ingenuity or thought they needed to revamp the part-time hiring practices; either way, the modified cubicle addressed the gap and allowed me to concentrate on the work.

Years later when I started at the city of Ontario, I found an American flag diffuser light panel that I could place over the standard translucent diffusers that would have really helped in Fountain Valley! After I bought and installed them myself, I once again created a line of fireman outside my little office nook, quick to take photos of the new guy in his unique setup. Lots of laughs. A few months later, then Deputy Chief Bob Snow apparently saw me carrying my personal projector back and forth from my car each day, and one Monday, I showed up at work with a brand new, top of the line projector on my desk. He swung by and said he couldn't believe I was transporting my home projector back and forth. His simple act of kindness made a significant impact on a challenging physical and environmental issue.

Unfortunately, the cardboard, diffusers, and new projectors couldn't solve all my light sensitivity problems. I still had to attend meetings and walk around these buildings, and the exposure was painful. There had to be a better solution. I scoured the internet and searched for a doctor in neuro-optometry. Ultimately, in 2015, after trying lots of different models with well-intentioned but unsuccessful neuro-optometry teams, I came across Dr. Valerie Quan at Western University School of Health Sciences in Pomona, California. After a thorough examination, Dr. Quan acknowledged that my light sensitivity was severe. My ability for my eyes to remain steady and focused in any environment due to the injury was limited, but a fluorescent-lit environment caused severe impairment and system shutdown. She said it was one of the worst cases she'd seen in her career.

I was digesting the depressing diagnosis when she said in a firm, reassuring voice that instilled all my trust, "I don't have the answers for you right now. I don't have the tool to make your life better, but I will search the world for the answers. We'll work together on this." This was the doctor-patient partnership I sought after. I leaned heavily on Dr. Quan, but I also started searching the world and looking for additional solutions to my visual impairment.

The solution was going to be a special pair of eyeglasses. While Dr. Quan and her team ran a battery of tests to determine the exact color lens that would compensate for my light sensitivity and alleviate the symptoms it caused, I searched for the appropriate frames. I found Theraspecs, a Southern California company built by Hart Shafer, whose wife had a light sensitivity disorder; necessity continues to be the mother of invention. I recognized that the frames he had invented were lightweight enough to be worn all day without causing a lot of physical strain on my nose and ears.

I purchased a pair of his frames, and Dr. Quan and her team mounted the lenses. For the first time in the years since my brain injury, I was able to sustain a full day under fluorescent lights, headache-free—reducing over 95 percent of my migraines. Though I had spent years trying one-size-fits-all solutions, only when Dr. Quan and her team worked with me to create a customized solution did I find relief. Light, however, isn't the only stimulus that overwhelms me.

FLOODING

The throbbing began behind my left eye, echoing the bass of the parade music as Mickey, Donald, and Pluto marched down Main Street next to Snow White and Dopey. Despite my sunglasses, the dancing, waving, colorful characters struck my eyes like brilliant, painfully psychedelic welding sparks. Conversations among people in the crowd sounded like Charlie Brown's teacher—even though I was at Disneyland—"wanh wah wanh wanh wah." The sights whirred and blurred around me, much like the effect of the Tea Cup ride earlier in the day. My wife Nicole noticed my glassy, glazed-over eyes and my slurred words. Having been through this countless times before, she knew my brain was flooding.

Flooding is fairly universal to brain injury patients and occurs when the brain—overwhelmed by external stimuli like bright, flashing lights, crowds, and dancing Disney characters—starts going through a process of shutting down. In my case, auditory processing gets slower, I'm unable to focus visually, and severe neurological fatigue sets in. The only way for me to reset is to lie down in a dark room, close my eyes, completely eliminate the external stimuli, and shut everything down. That day in Disneyland, Nicole sat me down on a bench in a quiet, shady corner of Toon Town and came back for me a few hours later. While I do my best to avoid over-stimulating situations that instigate flooding, in the first years after my brain injury, flooding caused disruption and interruption three or four times a week.

New managers won't have the neurological and physical reactions of someone with brain injury, but the emotional reaction to a new environment is similar. Taking a promotion or starting a new job can bring the same sensations of being overwhelmed by external stimuli. Newly promoted managers face a number of issues, challenges, and changing priorities on top of simply learning the layout of a new building and finding the bathrooms and water cooler. The first days after transitioning to a new position can feel like trying to drink from a fire hose.

When you know what you're getting into, you can plan

ahead and develop compensatory techniques. When my daughter was in kindergarten, she wanted me to accompany her to the father-daughter dance. Spending an evening in a dark, noisy auditorium with 150 kindergarteners is a situation I would normally avoid at all costs, but because attending the dance was important to my daughter, it was important to me.

Nicole and I worked out a series of strategies. I wore my dark sunglasses and ear plugs, and on the way to the event (arriving fashionably late), I convinced Leah to leave the dance early so we could be first in line at the frozen yogurt stand after the dance. Creating a strategy ahead of time gave me an exit plan when things started to escalate with flooding and made sure that my daughter felt that she was special. I made it to the father-daughter dance. We escaped early to get to our frozen yogurt, and as soon as I pulled in the driveway, Nicole met me outside. I kissed Leah on her head, and then I went to the bedroom, closed the door, and turned the lights off. By employing compensatory techniques, I've attended many father-daughter dances.

In the workplace, there are several approaches to thinking about the competing priorities and new challenges, issues, and complaints that you're expected to solve right away:

- Is there a strategy that will help cut down on the anxiety and stress of this current situation of transition and change?

- How much really needs to be compensated for?
- How much can be let go?
- How much is extraneous noise that doesn't have to be dealt with right now?

In each of my own job transitions, through the process of interviewing my boss to understand his priorities and expectations, and interviewing the team to understand their needs, I've been able to identify the top three to five things that I absolutely need to accomplish. I stay alert and focused on those projects by eliminating items which are neither urgent nor priorities.

If the new manager feels like he's flooding, it's important to develop compensatory techniques and counter with an action, such as:

- Changing the structure
- Changing the schedule
- Changing the tools
- Celebrating early victories

New managers tend to focus on the big picture and lose track of the small victories. If you want to quit after two weeks on the job, step back and take a realistic look at what's happened in those first two weeks. They may be small things like having a good meeting with a stakeholder or sharing a nice breakfast with the boss. Recognizing the small victories alleviates the feelings of failure and self-doubt and helps build the momentum and motivation to tackle big challenges.

In the end, preventing your version of flooding is about changing your mindset and seeing the situation through a different paradigm. Remember, every single person in the world who gets promoted and takes on a new job feels some level of anxiety and overwhelm. In moments like that, I remind myself that my boss has gone through this. My mentor has gone through this. My best friend went through this. This is a normal part of change and transition. But like Viktor E. Frankl, Austrian neurologist, psychiatrist, and Holocaust survivor, writes in his seminal work, *Man's Search for Meaning*, "Forces beyond your control can take away everything you possess except one thing, your freedom to choose how you will respond to the situation."

COMPENSATORY TECHNIQUES IN ACTION

Compensatory techniques are about taking a comprehensive approach to a gap or a deficit that the new leader, team, or organization has and not settling on a single approach. In the workplace, it's important to create as many chances for success as possible when tackling a challenge or learning a new skill.

EMPLOYEES WHO FLOOD

Watch for the hours the new employee is putting into the workplace. She may feel compelled to show the boss she's willing to go above and beyond by working an extraordinary number of hours, but if the employee starts out working sixty to seventy hours a week, that might not be sustainable in the long run. Working sixty to seventy hours a week leads to increased stress on relationships and the home front. It means less sleep, less physical fitness, and less leisure and relaxation.

Good managers do a few things when it looks like an employee is flooding:

- Let their employees know that while they appreciate the extra hours, they don't want the employee to sacrifice their family or health for the sake of the organization. They also assure the new employee that they have nothing to prove—they've already been promoted.

- Give them a book or resource that talks about work-life balance and the importance of having outside activities. I've gifted the book *The First 90 Days* to quite a few of my newly-promoted employees. Another favorite of mine is Tim Ferriss's *The 4-Hour Workweek*, which introduced me to lifestyle design and workplace efficiency.

- Communicate the value of vacations. Make sure they're scheduling time with their family and friends and planning some getaway time.

A new employee who floods out early and doesn't make it to the dance doesn't serve anyone. Having some of those conversations early on is important, as is making sure that they have systems and structures in place where they can capture priorities, the to-do list, and information.

We hired a twenty-two-year-old college graduate in our community services department to be an entry-level office assistant—her first job. All she had on her resume was the speech and debate team, a bachelor's degree, AP classes, and her GPA (PS: never put your GPA on a resume!). Two weeks after she started, she tendered her letter of resignation. The HR manager asked why she was resigning and if something had happened.

The assistant said, "Oh, no. The people are wonderful and outstanding. I had no idea what this office job would entail. I had no idea there'd be so much going on." I don't know if she didn't do her homework to understand the position, or if we failed to sit down with her on her first day to make sure she wouldn't feel so overwhelmed and flooded out that she had to resign. We probably could have done a better job as an organization to help her prepare and set up some tools and structures. She shouldn't have felt so overwhelmed that her *only* choice was to run to that dark room and turn off the lights.

The compensatory techniques I learned combined three parts:

- **Physical tools,** for example: a handheld voice recorder, whiteboard markers, or the Porta-Pottys for the SWAT team.
- **Practical techniques** or brain games, such as mnemonics.
- **People to lean on,** like Dr. Quan and her team.

All three elements, but especially the third (leaning on others) means being secure and self-aware enough to know that no one leader brings all of the answers and all the strengths to the table.

Mnemonic devices have been around since Plato and Aristotle were philosophizing in Athens. The ancient Greeks defined two types of memory: natural memory and artificial memory. Humans are born with the instinctual, natural memory, while artificial memory is learned. My brain injury took away much of my natural memory ability; brain school taught me artificial memory and mnemonics. Mnemonic devices are learning techniques that aid information retention or retrieval, the act of remembering in human memory.

When I was learning compensatory techniques in rehabilitation, I never dreamed that my colleagues and friends would want to steal them from me. In the second year of brain injury school, the rehab team thought it would be good for me to bring a friend or two with me to class, so they could identify and relate to what I was going through. I invited Tom, who I'd known since the first day of kindergarten. The first session of the day was about mnemonic devices. Tom has suffered from ADHD since he was a child. Staying focused in school had been difficult for him, and if there was a TV within Tom's vision, we'd have to shake him to grab his attention. After thirty minutes in my brain injury class, he said, "Why isn't everybody required to go to brain school?" He couldn't believe how much the techniques that he was learning would assist him with his daily challenges.

Forgetting someone's name isn't unique to brain injury. Most people complain they have trouble remembering names and that trouble is certainly exacerbated by brain injury. A normal human brain has trouble remembering anything that's fleeting or banal. There's nothing extraordinary about meeting someone on an airplane, which is why most people forget their seatmate's name by the time the plane lands. With a brain injury, even remembering deep encounters is complicated, let alone remembering fleeting encounters, because the injured brain doesn't create memory impressions as easily as a normal brain does.

Sometimes after a keynote speech during a breakout session or a Q&A segment, I'll ask a member of the audience a question and will ask their name before they speak. I pause for a moment and then allow them to ask their question. During the pause, I'm mentally creating a wacky, extreme way of remembering their name.

If the person's name is Lisa, for example, I'll look at her and visualize another Lisa I know from my past, ideally someone from my life before my brain injury when my memory was stronger. I'll remember Lisa, the gorgeous cheerleader from my high school, and then I'll add something that's visually extreme that begins with the same letter of her name, like a Lizard on Lisa's Left Leg. When I want to reference what Lisa said or if I see her by the doughnuts during the coffee break, I have a couple ways to remember her name: when I look at her, I see the Lisa I grew up with and I see a lizard on Lisa's Left Leg. It's a weird, extreme image that differentiates itself from my other memories and makes a mark on my brain. I will likely remember Lisa's name for at least the rest of the day, and the technique is so effective that sometimes I'll remember someone's name for several months after the encounter. Lisa with a Lizard on her Left Leg.

When a leader begins a new position, he's required to meet a lot of new people and mnemonic devices are a great compensatory technique to use to remember their names. For example, when a colleague named Fred speaks up at a team meeting, the new leader takes a moment to think of any Freds that he may know from his past. He can employ this mnemonic device, and now, every time he sees Fred in the workplace, the first thing he'll think about is a freckled face, just like Fred from second grade. It works extremely well to create a long-lasting memory and a connection.

When I've had to remember the names of many new people in the workplace, I've created flashcards. I've gone to the HR department, and asked them to print out their names and ID photos and used them to make flashcards. On the back of the flashcard, I wrote their name and an extreme sentence to create a mnemonic device tied to their name. I reviewed the flashcards on my own repeatedly; then, when I saw the new people around the office, I would smile or chuckle a little bit inside because I've associated their name with some sort of weird animal or disease. It's an extreme way of making an impression on my brain, but it works. While I learned these techniques out of necessity to compensate for my brain injury, they tend to be useful in the daily personal and professional lives of people without a brain injury.

The compensatory techniques I learned are useful in and of themselves. However, more important for workplace success is the process of developing compensatory techniques to fill the gaps or weaknesses in the team.

WHERE DID I LEAVE MY CAR?

One of the first activities I relearned with my rehabilitation team was navigating a list of errands and chores. The things humans do throughout their days more or less without thinking about them—getting groceries, doing laundry, and going to appointments—had become Herculean tasks for me. My occupational therapist, my physical therapist, my speech therapist, and my neuropsychologist helped me develop techniques that compensated for the functional deficits I sustained after the brain injury. The rehab team worked with me to figure out how I could successfully show up in a location, know what I was supposed to do, and keep my daily life and activities organized.

For example, in the early days after my brain injury, I wore a handheld voice recorder on my belt every single day. When I woke in the morning, I recorded a list of the things I needed to accomplish that day. If I was going to the supermarket, I'd write down the items I needed and then vocally record the list, in case I misplaced the written one. When I reached the grocery store, I'd record a note to myself about where I'd parked the car.

My post-injury brain has a really hard time remembering things that are routine. On a daily basis, I will put on deodorant multiple times because it's a routine task and my brain doesn't capture the memory of doing it. To make a memory, especially when you have a brain injury, but even if you don't, the task or name has to stand out and differentiate itself from the routine, which the brain ignores. When I go to the supermarket, I park in a spot lined up with a specific letter of the name on the storefront. For example, if I go to Sprouts, I'll intentionally park in line with the S. Then, I create a vivid, colorful sentence to remember, often using vulgar language or something extreme. Today, if I park at the S, the sentence might be "Sexy Samantha is stunning and sensational." I repeat the sentence a few times and may take a photo on my phone, which has in many ways replaced the recorder on my belt. My brain would latch on to the sentence and create an image. Coming out of the store, I'd be triggered by the sentence and remember my car was parked in line with the S.

I added a third technique to my voice recorder and mnemonics. Each night, I would write two things on the bathroom mirror with a dry erase pen: first, I'd write the first thing I had to do in the morning after my daily hygiene was complete; second, I'd write an affirmation or positive message to give me a little encouragement. My most used slogan is: "This too shall pass." Seeing these two things every morning helped me organize my day and move forward, regardless of the challenges ahead. Think about a positive affirmation you can keep next to your desk. What would you write on your mirror?

ONE IS GOOD—TWO IS BETTER

To get a good workout, a weightlifter doesn't do one exercise and say, "Wow, that was a great bicep workout. My arms are terrific." He does a series of exercises focused on the different arm muscles.

I began working as a dispatcher in September 2000, just shy of two years into rehabilitation, and my rehab team worked with me to develop techniques so that I could be an effective dispatcher. Dispatchers need to know the geography of the area they support. When they respond to a 911 call, dispatchers see the address from the display that shows the location of the caller, but the best dispatchers are able to mentally put themselves in the position of the caller and have a general sense of where they're sending the police officers or firefighters. Oftentimes a caller is confused about their exact location so the more familiar a dispatcher is with the area, the better they will be at determining the actual location of the emergency.

Not wanting to solely depend on the computer-provided address information, I created a series of laminated maps and drove around the territory our police department was responsible for, making notes on the laminated maps about landmarks such as key neighborhoods, major retail centers, parks, hazardous facilities, etc. I brought these laminated maps to work and placed them near my dispatch console. The maps became living documents that reinforced my mental picture of the area. At my dispatch console, I had the computer-provided information, a personal familiarity of where things were located in our service area from my excursions, and all my notes and drawings on those laminated maps.

If we are truly committed to embracing a cognitively diverse team and making sure all our employees feel welcome and able to bring their best self, we must be aware that people may require unique tools and resources to do their best, and solving a complex work challenge may require more than one approach. One of the most enjoyable parts of my job as the number two at the city of San Juan Capistrano is helping my boss, the organization's CEO, look at a complex problem from different angles. Even when Ben has strong feelings about how we should approach a complex policy or organizational issue, he will still call me in to his office to look at the problem from all angles, and we "try out" different solutions and weigh the ramifications. Even better is when he calls a few others into the huddle, those that really think differently from various levels of the organization, to poke holes in our gut response. The group always comes up with a much better resolution and because we've considered all the ramifications of various solutions, we are rarely surprised by the outcomes.

CHOOSE THE RIGHT WEAPON

The goal of brain school is to provide the patient with the groundwork for as many different compensatory techniques as possible and then to teach the patient to customize those techniques, so they can go to that tool belt for any situation that they confront.

When a police officer is sent on patrol in the community, he's isn't told, "Here's your gun. Use it to take care of everything you come across." The officer is equipped with a firearm, a backup firearm, handcuffs, pepper spray, a baton, a Taser, a shotgun, a rifle, even a sap back in the day! Officers are given a myriad of diverse tools and lots of options and know to apply the proper tool to the right situation. Much of an officer's training in the academy is focused on tools not worn on the belt, things like tactical communication, interrogation tactics, and other soft skills that may be more effective than the gun belt.

The tools aren't limited to one type each. For example, there are different types of batons. Every police officer learns the fundamentals of what a baton does and the situations where a baton the is most effective, then when the time comes, every officer decides which one to use. Some officers have straight sticks, some officers have PR 24s, others have ASPs that collapse and expand. Some officers don't carry a baton at all. One officer I know leaves his baton in the car and only uses it for riot control. Yet another uses nunchucks (sometimes referred to as nunchaku) for more of a pain compliance approach (less Bruce Lee). As Greg Mayer, a retired Los Angeles police captain and an expert on use of force, says in an interview with CNN[2], "The challenge is to find and adopt equipment and tactics that get the job done but cause the fewest and least severe injuries to suspects and officers."

---

2   Michael Martinez, Dan Simon, Augie Martin, "Nunchucks, popularized by Bruce Lee, come to California police agency," CNN (November 4, 2015). https://www.cnn.com/2015/11/04/us/california-police-equipment-nunchucks/index.html

Each individual must personalize their technique, so they can use it easily and comfortably and use the right tool for the right job.

VISUAL LEARNERS

The emergency manager on my staff, Lynn, came into my office and said, "Can you help me understand how to write this agenda report for the council meeting?" I began explaining that there are sections of a council meeting called "calendars" and different items go into different sections. Before I finished my sentence, I had created a visual representation of the council meeting sections on the dry erase board. Other leaders may have remained seated at their desk and explained the agenda report, but my brain needs a visual representation both to absorb new information and to teach clearly.

It's common for people with brain injuries to rely on pictures and visuals to learn and communicate. Just as people are cognitively diverse, they also learn in different ways. Some people are visual learners who need to see an image to understand new material. Other people learn audibly and can remember instructions for a task simply by listening to someone explain the steps. Others can read a passage once and retain the details in the recesses of their brain. Many people retain information more effectively when at least two of their sensory inputs are combined, and it's even better when meaning is attached to the memory or the item at hand. For example, watching someone perform a new task while they explain how the task is done or reading new material that's accompanied by charts or photos is great, but even better is developing an association. For example, when teaching Lynn about the components of the agenda report, I explained the sections, drew a visual on the dry erase board, explained why the report would fall under each section, even using examples from her former career to help her reach the fullest understanding.

Just as a brain injury patient needs to make sure there are multiple strategies learned and applied, the manager or leader also needs to know that there are multiple strategies and ways that the team will connect with, learn, and implement new material. The most effective managers are able to look at their teams and try to figure out different ways to inspire and train them to be the most effective.

HELPING EMPLOYEES GROW

Instead of asking the employee, "Why can't you understand this?" The emotionally intelligent manager asks, "how can I help you understand this in a different way?" The boss asks themselves, "Where am I falling short in providing my colleague with the tools, resources, and the motivation to take ownership and move forward? What can I do to present this information differently? What can I do to help them learn this material?"

Employees certainly don't go to their bosses and say, "Hey boss, I suck at this," however, they might say, "I need help." Because of my brain injury, I'm comfortable talking about weaknesses and gaps. After all, I had to spend years immersed in learning what was damaged and what could be done to compensate. That should always lead to a conversation about how to fill the gap and implement the tool or strategy.

I once had my human resources director ask if the city would pay for an executive coach. At first, I was thrown off. She's innovative, dynamic, and highly competent and after all, I'm a great boss, right? So, why would she need to seek guidance elsewhere? Well, that was a self-absorbed response to her inquiry. It didn't take but a few moments for me to stop that wasteful train of thought and understand that she was just fully committed to ensuring that she was growing and improving. She thought she could become an even better leader and better help her team deal with the increasing work load if she had a neutral party to bounce her ideas off of. She brought both the problem and the solution to me, and I appreciated and immediately approved of her desire to learn, grow, and improve. Coaches aren't commonplace in the public sector, but every great leader should take advantage of executive coaches for both themselves and their key team members.

When the manager doesn't create an environment where people are encouraged to embrace tools and resources to account for gaps and challenges, it actually creates more of a dependency on others. In a non-growth environment, the employee may pass a duty off to someone else rather than think about developing the compensatory technique that will enable him to do it.

COMPARTMENTALIZE CHALLENGES

As a result of my brain injury, I had to learn to compartmentalize immediately. All brain injury patients in rehab are in some level of pain because of the physical injury and have to be able to compartmentalize defeat. For me, light sensitivity was an overwhelming challenge. If I had let it consume me and focused only on staying in the dark as much as possible, I wouldn't have been able to spend any energy on the other areas of brain injury rehabilitation that I needed to work through. By compartmentalizing or putting the current issue or source of challenge in a nice, tidy, confined box, I learned to make that one overwhelming challenge just one of many—giving it less power. Dealing with my light sensitivity occupied a lot of my time in rehabilitation. Compartmentalizing allowed me to focus on solving other challenges, too.

As a result of brain injury rehab, I can quickly switch from one issue to another. For example, I could have a minor fender bender on my way to work, but when I reach the office, I can focus on the priorities of the workday. It's a technique to ensure that one element doesn't take me down. This skill was likely reinforced as a police dispatcher where I had to handle a crisis one moment, and then rapidly switch to helping someone locate their lost cat the next.

In the workplace, managers are confronted by many different challenges and need to make sure they're not completely consumed by one challenge. Compartmentalization can help. Once the challenge has been named and defined from all angles, compartmentalization means taking control of the situation and not letting one challenge change the trajectory of every other task.

Compartmentalization helps leaders set priorities. Those conversations with the boss, peers, and subordinates help identify the challenges that are urgent and those that are important but have lower priority. If they assume that all tasks are equal in their deadlines and urgency, leaders can choose to tackle the challenges that will bring the greatest reward first and use that momentum to take on the next set of challenges. In a nutshell:

- Consider whether the overwhelming challenge is

urgent or important, so you can assign it the proper priority.

- Acknowledge that the challenge is overwhelming and look for ways to break it into smaller, more manageable pieces.
- Focus on a few things that can be successfully and satisfactorily completed; momentum builds by solving smaller issues.

Compartmentalization can be of real benefit in the workplace when dealing with change and confronting a whole new environment. Panic is a common emotional reaction to change. Leaders can mentor employees by teaching them to compartmentalize that which they're struggling with and put it in its rightful place, using the right amount of effort, energy, and skill with consideration of priority and urgency. When employees use compartmentalization, challenges are faced from a rational, cognitive place rather than from an emotional place. By not getting too excited about any one thing, they can stay on track with multiple demands. They become active participants in deciding how the challenge can be dealt with.

BRING IT TO THE MIDLINE

"Cling tooth and nail to the following rule: not to give in to adversity, never to trust prosperity, and always take full note of fortune's habit of behaving just as she pleases, treating her

as if she were actually going to do everything it is in her power to do. Whatever you have been expecting for some time comes as less of a shock."

—SENECA, *LETTERS FROM A STOIC*

A strategy I learned in brain injury school from my counselor Kim Peterson is related to compartmentalization. Emotions and reactions are often extreme in brain injury patients. Good news can bring on a heightened euphoria, while bad news can be devastatingly depressing and, at times, make us question moving forward. Kim, in teaching us about handling extreme emotions, would say, "Bring it to the midline." The midline is an acceptable range, and it's not about killing off enthusiasm or excitement, but about staying in that range. If a brain injury patient can come back from an extremely high level to the midline, that trains his brain to also come back to the midline from an extremely low level, avoiding feelings of impending doom.

With compartmentalization, the secret is making sure that any one thing doesn't overwhelm and disable the manager. The workplace is fraught with challenges and issues, some big and some small. The manager needs to have the self-awareness and control to say, "No, this is not going to overtake me. I'm going to deal with some other things with success to build a sense of accomplishment, then when I return to the challenge, it won't seem so overwhelming."

If one hundred of my former employees were asked, "What don't you like about Jacob?" They would probably answer, "It's the same thing we admire—he's radically direct." I am able to compartmentalize and avoid the catastrophic emotional response. I also share with my staff that when they don't receive direct feedback from me, assume all is well, as I would share my concerns if I had any. Because I respect my team, I love them enough to be honest with them. I brought the non-emotional response I had to use when I was a dispatcher to all my subsequent positions. Being a dispatcher taught me good business skills, but I was a great dispatcher because I had a brain injury.

Compartmentalization allows me to leave my personal life and health issues outside of the workplace. Many of my closest coworkers have no idea that I have Crohn's disease and have functioned at work after surgeries and hospitalizations (sometimes with open wounds and embarrassing physical challenges), and some still think I wear sunglasses inside to be cool. Compartmentalizing allows me to continue forward with positive movement. I'm not strapped down by pain and anguish; I give the physical challenges the attention they deserve and move on. It comes down to taking control of a situation. Compartmentalization is empowering and enables a tangible, practical outcome. If done properly, it provides a lot of strength to handle challenging situations.

Leaders need to create an environment for their teams where they know that they can come to you, not with a problem but with recommended solutions, and that you, as a manager, are going to give those recommendations fair consideration, support the tools required, and create an environment where challenges are welcomed and not avoided. Ultimately, this creates an authentic environment which allows the team to dominate and transcend previous barriers.

CHAPTER 5

WEAR YOUR SUNGLASSES

"There is much talk of authentic leadership, being yourself. Perhaps it is even more important that leaders focus on enabling others to be themselves."

—ALISON REYNOLDS AND DAVID LOUIS,
HARVARD BUSINESS REVIEW

After my brain injury, I was in a six-month home-based rehabilitation program in Berkeley. Other than my parents, my roommates were the only two people who knew I'd dropped out of Berkeley and was in full-time rehab; it was hard to hide it from them with occupational therapists, speech therapists, physical therapists, and other healthcare providers knocking on the door each day. I told the rest of the world I was a full-time student. I didn't want to talk about myself or my situation because I had no idea who I was. I'd lost everything I'd based my identity on up to the day of the attack. To maintain my lie, whenever I met with friends I pretended I was a full-time student with only typical student problems, never mentioning medical challenges or brain injury. I later learned I'd done a terrible job faking my student identity; my closest friends didn't know what exactly was wrong with me, but it was clear to them that I was not being truthful.

Every few months I flew to Southern California to visit my family—like a normal student would do. Prior to my injury, I looked forward to flying. It gave me a sense of independence. Pre-injury, when the small talk with my seatmate reached the "what do you do?" question, I proudly answered that I was a student at UC Berkeley, studying international relations to someday create world peace as a diplomat. The conversation that ensued about my studies and future plans validated my self-worth and self-esteem, and I found comfort in knowing that not only did I enjoy the path I was pursuing, but others perceived my path as the right path.

Post-injury, it was the question I dreaded. I was terrified to give the honest answer: "I'm a full-time patient." I feared that at best, my seatmate would ask to be moved for fear of catching something from me; at worst, they would call the attendant to take me away. The social interaction that I'd so enjoyed on flights became an anxiety-ridden drama.

On one particular flight, my ticket placed me in the final boarding call, and when I reached the airplane, only a middle seat remained. The gentleman occupying the window seat was upwards of 300 pounds; his leg and arm were dominating the vacant middle seat, but that seat was my only choice. I was more concerned about the pending "what do you do?" than about his size. I asked if the seat was available. He said, "Yes," and then began apologizing for his size. "I'm sorry you drew the short straw." He seemed anxious and said "Can you fit? My name is Miles. It's nice to meet you, and I'm glad to see a friendly face here on the flight." Immediately, my anxieties about the obligatory conversation subsided. His admission of his own insecurities lessened my own.

As the plane took off, I realized that he looked familiar, and I thought I recognized him from one of those extreme MTV reality shows of the late 1990s. I said, "I'm sorry to ask this, but you look familiar. Do I know you?" He said, "I don't think we know each other, but I'm on a TV show so perhaps that's why you recognize me." Then he turned the conversation back to me and asked, "How are you feeling today? How are you doing?" Not, "what do you do?"

He put me at ease, and for the next ninety minutes, we had a great conversation, returning my enjoyment of flying and forgetting how much work it took to hide who

I was. We talked about everything—things I hadn't been able to discuss with my closest friends—the injury, rehab, the doctors, and the challenges I was facing. When he opened the conversation with his own insecurities, he gave me permission to be myself and enjoy a genuine connection with another human being.

When leaders openly talk about whatever terrifies them or causes anxiety, they give permission to everyone around them to do the same.

BRING YOUR BEST SELF

I was in a meeting with a well-known business owner in Ontario, and the pain of my migraine felt like a needle being pushed out from behind my left eye. Over the next twelve to twenty-four hours, the needle became a jackhammer, pounding on my left temple until the left side of my face went numb. All-consuming nausea ensued. Despite having a tool to avoid the pain, I kept my sunglasses in my bag during that meeting. It was easier to experience the pain and discomfort than to be the odd man out in a room of colleagues and those I was trying to impress.

When I put the sunglasses on, I felt instantly relieved, but I was also placing something between myself and the world. I was cognizant of the impact that had on people around me. When I was out in the world I could feel people staring at me, and I imagined their judgmental thoughts: "Who does this guy think he is? Why is he wearing sunglasses indoors?" I felt awkward, uncomfortable, and embarrassed. I was supposed to wear the sunglasses all day in my work environment, in meetings, while talking about difficult topics with employees, and in team building sessions. Ultimately, especially in my work environment, I often hid my sunglasses.

The downside was that I spent a lot of my energy compensating for the pain and the nausea and just trying to get through my day. I tried to compartmentalize my work, but even this usual go-to strategy wasn't enough on its own, and I was missing a lot of what was going on. Hiding the pain kept me from relating effectively with others. Hiding my sunglasses, however, meant I wasn't showing up as who I was. Either way, I created a disconnect between myself and the outside world. The shame, anxiety, and discomfort impeded my ability to have deep and meaningful relationships in the workplace and they were an obstacle to success, too.

That's exactly the opposite of what leaders want to achieve in the workplace. Leaders want to have strong, deep, and effective connections with colleagues and staff. They want team members to trust them. They want to be able to influence new people and create a connection that's authentic.

Although I had my compensatory technique in my brief-case, I only used it when no one would see me or in situations where sunglasses were more appropriate. I wasn't using the tool that solved my own gap, and I prevented my own high performance and achievement. How could I expect my team to bring their best selves to work if I wasn't doing so myself? I thought my sunglasses created a barrier, but the truth was, not wearing the sunglasses created a blockade. I spent so much energy hiding who I was, I didn't have any energy leftover to be the authentic me.

I'M NOT BONO

When I'm giving a keynote speech, I come out on stage wearing my green sunglasses—because, generally, the lighting conditions in most hotels and event venues have some sort of fluorescence—but I don't address the elephant in the room for the first twenty minutes. Then I say to the audience, "I've been talking for twenty minutes, and I'll bet something about me has been distracting most of you the whole time." A slide of Bono and Yoko Ono appears on the screen and laughter fills the room.

I'm not Bono, nor have I ever been mistaken for Yoko Ono. I ask the audience for a show of hands of those who have been so distracted trying to figure out why I wear sunglasses that they hadn't heard a word I'd said so far.

Most of the people in the room raise their hand. I then ask for one courageous volunteer to share what he or she was thinking. Common answers include: "I thought you were trying to be cool," "I thought you were hungover," "I thought you were being an ass," or "I thought you were blind until I saw you maneuver around the tables." When I ask how many people had formed a negative impression of me because I was wearing sunglasses, again, most of the hands in the room go up. After wearing my sunglasses for many years, I'm used to this type of reaction.

In the keynote presentations, I have a platform to explain that I wear sunglasses to block the light that causes debilitating migraines that are a residual effect of my brain injury. I share that I feel all of those impressions and my own insecurities often kept my sunglasses in my bag. At work, I kept my reasons to myself—until I decided to share my story.

FULL DISCLOSURE

While I was at the city of Ontario, the human resources department working with the city manager developed a leadership program called LINKS. Each month, executives in the organization met with a cohort of fifteen people who held the position of supervisor or higher. Executives met with a different cohort each month, and the executive decided how to spend the scheduled two hours with the cohort, as long as it was something that helped the cohort develop professionally.

After being promoted to an executive position and sitting on the other side of the table as the presenter, I decided to tell my story to each cohort about the attack, rehabilitation, and the subsequent search for the proper sunglasses. In a dozen years of working in the public sector, I had never shared my story. The professional development part would come through in the lessons I'd learned from my experience and how I applied those lessons to my professional journey.

In the first meeting, about half of the fifteen people in the room were people who I'd supervised or worked closely with. As I told my story, jaws in the room literally dropped. The people who'd worked most closely with me had no idea I wore my sunglasses for medical reasons. For years, my closest colleagues thought I was trying to make a fashion statement. Police officers with whom I'd spent many middle-of-the-night call outs thought I wore sunglasses to be cool. I had always assumed people knew I wore sunglasses for medical reasons.

An interesting thing happened. No one in the group responded negatively. We felt an instant connection, like the bond I would feel with my fellow dispatchers and officers after a particularly difficult and high-stress call. For the first time in many years of public service, I felt genuine acceptance and connection from everyone in the room. More importantly, I saw in their eyes that while they focused on my story, they were also identifying situations and insecurities in their own life that had held them back in their work environment. Their nodding heads told me I had reached a deep place.

I tapped into the discovery that leaders must be humans first for our teams. When leaders only show strength and infallibility, they create a barrier between themselves and their team. When leaders make themselves vulnerable, they create deeper, tighter, more meaningful connections. When the leader starts to disclose areas in which he feels he has a weakness, he gives the team an opportunity to compensate for the leader's weakness.

At the end of the two-hour meeting, the group didn't want to leave, although I told them several times our session was finished. They wanted to engage with each other and continue to talk about their own challenges. They wouldn't clear the room! I began to hear their stories. One of the city's newer employees, Jill, rose from her seat and began walking toward me. She walked with a slight limp. I asked her for her impression of the meeting. Her eyes were glassy with tears and she said, "Thank you so much, Jacob." She went on to say that she'd had a stroke before joining our team. In the two and a half years that she'd been in her present job, she'd never told anyone about her experience or why she walked with a limp.

She said, "Today I learned that you're messed up, and I'm messed up, and we can be messed up together!" We both laughed. She continued, "And it's all right, and it's not going to be a big deal." Her face brightened as she shared her insight. I was overcome with a tremendous sense of fulfillment. Everything that I'd gone through—the brain injury, rehabilitation, overcoming challenges—was worth it in that moment.

More than sharing your secrets with the world, vulnerability is recognizing that everyone has challenges and gaps. When you acknowledge, define, and address your own challenges, they become controllable instead of controlling. Recognizing your challenges and gaps becomes a strength that brings a whole series of benefits to the team, the organization, and you.

Each time I led a cohort, I shared my story and the result was always the same. After a few years of the program, I heard hundreds of stories from colleagues and coworkers. A burly police officer told me he suffered in shame with dyslexia on a daily basis. I couldn't help but wonder if he'd built his tough exterior to compensate and protect himself. When he shared his story with me, however, I could see that he'd made a discovery and that he would be able to tap into his experience and use it in the future. Once after giving a keynote speech, a gentleman who'd been a rising star in the host company confessed that he had a physical malformation. While rarely visible to others, he said it still causes him a lot of shame. He, like so many, thanked me for sharing my story and making it safe for him to share his story with someone for the first time.

The challenges that had made a detrimental impact on their lives and had held them back became strengths once they were finally disclosed. Rather than seeing the gaps as weaknesses, they were seen as experiences that added color, character, and perspective. My colleagues began to look at their own traumas and experiences as lessons to share with one another.

We were building authenticity. Talking about difficult things leads to a high level of connection, natural bonding, and mutual understanding. Celebrated author and researcher Dr. Brené Brown says, "Vulnerability is the birthplace of innovation, creativity, and change." And if you haven't yet seen her TED talks on the subject, play one of them at your next management meeting.

I left my sunglasses in my bag because I wanted to fit in. Human tendency is to want to be one with the crowd. Leaders have to know that peer pressure in the workplace is real, and peer pressure prevents people from wearing their sunglasses, and therefore, peer pressure prevents the creation of a resilient team performing at the highest level.

PROCESSING

The last hour of the day in brain school is called processing. It's the time when everyone brings their challenges to the group.

The skill of processing, simply put, is learning to share your challenges and, more importantly, becoming comfortable leaning on the guidance of others. Before my injury, I was an academic achiever and community leader. I was kicked off that bar stool and hit the ground hard. I had to learn how to lean in order to figure out how to get back up.

In brain injury processing, the insight and guidance that is given is because we have each other's best interests in mind. We want each other to be successful when we go out and interact with the rest of the world.

The workplace rarely offers a structured time for this type of discussion, feedback, and input about things that aren't specific to a project.

One company I worked with incorporated a process of "open office hours," where functional teams met on a regular basis to discuss organizational and interpersonal challenges, not necessarily tied to a specific project. This type of exchange helps employees build self-awareness, emotional intelligence, and creates a more cohesive unit. In addition, the meeting was an opportunity for people to share their best practices from prior experiences that may enhance the individuals, the current methodologies, and the organization.

What are you doing to create an environment where employees can build their emotional intelligence and seek feedback from others?

CONSTANT PURSUIT OF COGNITIVE DIVERSITY

As much as the leader should create a team of people that is cognitively diverse, he should also expose himself to different perspectives to make sure he doesn't become complacent.

In November 2015, I received a scholarship from the International City Management Association, ICMA, to represent the United States, along with two other individuals, in an exchange program with the New Zealand city management association called SLGM, the Society of Local Government Managers. The scholarship provided me with an opportunity to travel to New Zealand for two weeks and study leadership within their council-manager form of government. I took the opportunity to also immerse myself in the town of Christchurch, decimated from the 2010 and 2011 earthquakes, so that I could learn as many lessons as possible from New Zealand and from that earthquake experience.

I had the opportunity to look at local government leadership from the perspective of a country with a different history than the United States. The trip gave me many insights and new ways of approaching local government leadership, all of which I brought back to California. I was able to teach my colleagues about responding to major catastrophic events, as well as general leadership, team dynamics, and organizational structure. I still think about the Kiwi way of solving problems (heavy on the technology and seeking outside innovation approach) when dealing with public policy issues in my work today.

Leaders should always be looking for opportunities to learn from others and put themselves in situations that are uncomfortable. They have the responsibility to seek out ways to grow and see things from others' perspectives.

LIMITED DISCLOSURE

People often have an initial resistance to all this discussion about revealing weaknesses and blind spots. They flinch a little when I suggest talking about their insecurities in the workplace. I guarantee, however, the investment of energy and time is worth it. Once the leader embraces this concept of cognitive diversity, builds the right team, and makes sure that everybody feels like they're in an environment where they can wear their sunglasses, the outcome is an authentic work environment, where everybody brings all of their tools to the table to tackle whatever the challenges are.

I'm not advocating that leaders walk into the workplace and announce in the board room that they're insecure about the birthmark on the back of their left leg. I'm not suggesting leaders call an all-hands meeting with a thousand employees and tell them they were the victim of abuse. I don't want to turn the workplace into an episode of Dr. Phil.

I am saying it's important that leaders and managers let people be themselves in the workplace and embrace their differences, because those differences allow other people to be superheroes. As I mentioned earlier, research shows that the teams that are the most successful at dealing with change and challenges are those that have a diversity of knowledge and perspective, a diversity of background, and skill sets that are actually different.

When I finish a memo and take it to my boss, Ben, I think I've written an A+ quality paper. Instead, after he reads it, there's red ink all over the page. My report is one hundred times better with his changes. He sees what I can't see. He brings a mastery of editing and the English language. If I embrace his talent and skill, my product is better. If I am intimidated and insecure, I may not ask for his input. The document will be okay, but not great.

I'm proposing that leaders allow people the comfort of knowing that they can be different in the workplace, and they won't be rejected because of their differences. Their differences will provide the key value for the organization's or team's success.

MAKE THE CALL

Nobody embraced authenticity like Deputy Fire Chief Raymond (Ray) Ramirez. When I was hired by Fire Chief Chris Hughes, he told me, "Jacob, you have an important role. Walk ten steps behind Ray. Makes sure he gets to his meetings on time and learn everything you can from him."

Ray was the fire deputy chief, a reserve sheriff's deputy, and a lawyer. He always carried a book and a highlighter, and I don't think he spoke one word to me during my first week on the job. He's a brilliant man of few words who was always true to who he was and what he believed was right. He was consistent and predictable, humble, and all-in. Everyone at the fire department was better because of the strengths, the talents, and the wisdom that he brought to the table.

One night in October 2005 after leaving a comedy club, my wife Nicole noticed her throat was irritated after a night of laughing. She noticed a small bump in her throat and thought her vocal chords were just strained. After a week of trying to ignore the discomfort, she went to the doctor to get it examined. Four weeks, several specialists, and many probing exams, surgeries, and biopsies later, she called me at work, sobbing hysterically. "The doctor just called," she said, "he said it's cancer, Hodgkin's Lymphoma, and I have to go in tomorrow morning." I told her I'd come home right away.

I'd handled many hysterical callers during my time at the dispatch desk and had no problem maintaining control, but in this situation, I was in total shock. I went to Ray and said, "I just got a phone call from Nicole. She's at work, and the doc called her and says it's cancer. I have to go." He said, "Get out of here."

I'd been working for Ontario Fire for less than five months, we'd been married just over a year, and it had been a year of looking forward to the future. When I got home, I found

Nicole sobbing on the couch. There was no manual for how to handle a cancer diagnosis. No playbook, no checklist for what I was supposed to do as a spouse, how I was supposed to respond, or how to notify our family members—just complete shock and helplessness. After more crying, there was silence. I called our parents, our sisters, and her best friends. I wanted to create a village of support. Those calls were short; more tears from each call on the other end, and then silence again in our small apartment. Do we eat dinner? What more can I say to Nicole? Do I go to work tomorrow? What do I tell my boss? What should I share with my colleagues? Will they fire me if I attend Nicole's doctor's appointments?

At about 8 p.m. that night, my phone rang. It was Ray.

He said, "Hey, Jacob, it's Ray. I want to tell you something. I want you to focus on Nicole right now. I want you to know that we'll take care of everything that you have going on here at the department. Everybody in the Ontario Fire Department is behind you, is here for you, and will do anything for you. Your only assignment is to take care of your wife." Those were the exact words I needed to hear in that moment.

Most of the time, we don't call the person impacted by tragedy. We tell ourselves, "I don't want to make them feel uncomfortable. I don't want to bother them right now. I'll call when things settle down. I'll reach out later." Ray's call eliminated all the stress, pressure, and weight of the world so I could focus on the crisis at hand.

Everybody maintains that approach and what happens in the hours and days following a crisis is deafening silence. From my experience of going through my brain injury, Crohn's disease, Nicole's cancer, and other life losses, I believe people need to hear a supportive voice. They need to feel that they're not alone, that a village surrounds them. They won't accept the call if they can't talk at that moment, but later, hearing a voicemail that says, "Hey, this is your boss. I just want to let you know we're here for you. We're thinking about you," can give them the strength they need in that difficult time.

The leader may be the only one making that call. In the long run, the call reinforces the expectation of direct communication. It tells the team member that no matter how difficult the conversation, no matter how difficult the moment, no matter the level of chaos or the challenge, communication lines will remain open. The call says, "We are in this together, and while we may fear the crisis, we will not fear talking about it."

For the rest of my career, I could go into Ray's office, close the door, and talk to him about anything that needed to be discussed. Most wouldn't believe that someone as academic as Ray would be the model of communication and empathy, but Ray's actions that day demonstrated his commitment to communication in difficult situations. Years later, the department leaned on Ray to advocate for the needs of the organization during challenging leadership times, while many were silent. Ray taught me direct communication is compassionate leadership.

CHAPTER 6

IMPROVE WORKPLACE CULTURE

In 2006, *Inc.* magazine published an article written by Tony Hsieh, the CEO of Zappos, about his utilization of work culture as a way to positively impact his workforce. Two years later, Hsieh was featured on *Nightline* in a story called "Zappos Company Culture" that caught my attention. Hsieh spoke about a different way to work. He explained that if you invested in creating a culture that was respectful, engaging, and fun for your employees, a culture to which they connected, and also gave them the freedom to build and expand upon that culture, it could lead to exceptional customer service. Culture, therefore, impacted the relationship with your customers and could improve sales and profits. Hsieh's ideas spoke to a better way of doing business, work, and work culture. His ideas energized and inspired me. The news story also mentioned that Zappos welcomed visitors to witness and learn about their culture.

In late 2008, I was recovering from a major resection surgery to treat the Crohn's disease. I was having a difficult recovery, and my local doctors couldn't seem to pinpoint and resolve the problem. My friend Rob mentioned that his father-in-law was a specialist in Las Vegas who might be able to help resolve the complicated recovery I was experiencing. I decided to kill the proverbial two birds with one stone and go to Las Vegas to visit both the doctor and Zappos. I thought I might learn some tips to boost the work culture in the police department, even though I was likely the only police department employee visiting a shoe company for professional development guidance.

I called Zappos and learned that they were hosting tours five days a week. If I let them know the name of my hotel, the Zappos van would pick me up and take me to the Zappos headquarters, where I would take a three-hour tour of Zappos. And it was all free. I didn't hesitate to book my flight and hotel room and schedule my doctor's appointments.

I went to Las Vegas in May 2009, eight weeks after my

second major resection surgery. Travelling was physically challenging. I had open wounds and carried a backpack full of medical supplies. Every few hours I had to find a restroom to clean the wounds and take care of things. I was all-consumed by the physical challenges of the day until the moment I walked into Zappos headquarters. At that moment, all my stressors seemed to fade away, and I became immersed in a new world. I felt like Charlie in the Chocolate Factory meeting Willie Wonka for the first time. I felt like I belonged—and I wasn't even an employee. I could feel the positive work culture as soon as I walked through that door. Each person I met welcomed and accepted me.

Who wouldn't be energized? During the next two hours, my bureaucratic government brain was revolutionized. As I walked through each division in the Zappos company headquarters, every single person waved without being prompted, "Hello, how are you? Welcome to Zappos. Nice to have you here." The authenticity resonated from every division, from sales and customer service to human resources, finance, and IT.

Each employee was passionate about their area of responsibility; both their work area and the physical area they occupied. Customized cubicles reflected each individual's uniqueness, yet it all gelled together; no single cubicle stood out in a negative way. Countless employees waited for an opportunity to explain their history with the company and the symbolism of their decorative choices. While every person was different, they belonged to the larger organization that totally embraced authenticity and allowed them to be themselves. It wasn't simply about having "fun" in the workplace, it was a total commitment to work being done with an environment created to inspire and keep the workforce bonded to each other and the company.

I thought to myself, "Why aren't we creating this in government?"

In my own workplace at the police department, I struggled daily with my own differences. The awkward models of sunglasses I wore at the time served as a daily reminder of the ways I was different, not to mention my silent and self-conscious approach to the open wounds, bandages, and medical supplies that I had to carry around with me. While touring Zappos, I understood how the government approach that embraced white walls and flickering fluorescent lights could be giving our stakeholders the wrong impression of who we were and—perhaps, a greater detriment—did a disservice to our own employees. I didn't want the Zappos tour to end, and I felt an urgency to rethink local government employee engagement. Like Hsieh said, "For me, my role is about unleashing what people already have inside them that is maybe suppressed in most work environments."[3]

The last stop of the tour was the Zappos library, which held shelves lined with business and leadership books that their employees enjoyed and recommended to others. It's a generous library that offers forty or so copies of each book. Visitors were left to peruse the books, and the guide said, "Tony would like you to take as many of these books as you like. Put them in your bag, take them with you, and enjoy them just as our employees have enjoyed reading them and being inspired by them." I left Zappos with a dozen brand-new business books to continue the inspiration that I'd felt on the tour. The tour guide also gave me the *Zappos Culture Yearbook*, which collected unedited thoughts about the company from every employee.

In 2009, employees loved working at Zappos and people were pounding on the door to get a job there. Interestingly, Hsieh paid below market rate because he understood that people weren't primarily motivated by salary. Zappos and Hsieh were among the first to decide that work culture is where you should invest your time as a leader. Today, we may think of this as ping-pong tables and soda machines, but while these amenities existed at Zappos, it wasn't about the "fun"; it was about creating a work culture that

---

3   Asad Meah, "35 Inspirational Tony Hsieh Quotes On Success," AwakenTheGreatnessWithin. https://awakenthegreatnesswithin.com/35-inspirational-tony-hsieh-quotes-on-success/

allowed connectivity and a commitment to service. Hsieh understood that if your people feel connected in the culture, then your people will take care of the customer. In turn, your stakeholders will feel loyal to the organization because they will feel like they are being taken care of by people who really enjoy service.

The police department had a lot to learn from Zappos. When I returned, I was inspired to bring elements from Zappos to the police department and work them into the strategic process. I wanted to give employees a sense of ownership of their culture and give them a fun, enjoyable, and fulfilled work environment.

START WITH THE ENVIRONMENT

When I took on the role of police administrative director in the Ontario Police Department, the nickname for the dispatch center was the "snake pit"—it's no wonder the dispatchers had a culture problem that resulted in occasional service lapses and employees who lacked pride in their work. I returned from Zappos enthusiastic and driven by what I'd seen there. I had to lead the dispatchers to do something no other dispatch center had done, something that would build their pride and gain them respect from the other departments.

I created a plan that accomplished the two goals of giving

the dispatchers a reason to take pride in their work and overhaul the culture.

First, I evacuated the dispatch center for ten days. I broke everyone into teams, with each team responsible for moving a part of the dispatch center into a community room, a trailer, or the parking lot. No one had ever operated a dispatch center in evacuation circumstances. This drill prepared the dispatchers for an emergency and proved they could function in a remote center.

The second part of my plan was to secretly overhaul the physical environment of the dispatch center while the dispatchers were doing their ten-day evacuation. Changing the physical environment would allow them to see culture change.

I went to all the departments I knew in the city and asked them for any leftover equipment or material they could donate to the new dispatch center. IT provided displays, Public Works had some carpet, and another department provided paint. What's more, I explained to the other departments that the dispatchers were unappreciated, and I wanted all of us to show them gratitude.

After ten days of operating in remote locations and not missing any calls, the dispatchers walked back into a new center. I'd removed the pony wall barriers between the consoles and installed clean consoles with a nameplate for each dispatcher. The "snake pit" now had clean carpet and smelled of fresh paint.

We then set up a system of three metrics—data collection points—to test our ability for how fast we answered calls for service and how fast we sent officers to calls. If we met or exceeded our division goals, dispatchers could do personal tasks; doing crafts like quilting and sewing, or studying for a bachelor's degree in the dispatch center when the work was slow. From the outset, stats were off the charts every single month. The center operated as best in show.

When a manager takes over a division and knows performance is a problem, he knows some overhaul needs to take place. After the exploratory phase discussed in chapter two, the first step to improvement is to assess the physical environment and seek an opportunity to improve the conditions for the team. People need to *see* change. It's not enough that they hear about it or read about it in a memo. They may need to see the color of the walls change and help create an environment that supports achievement. Behavior will follow the physical change in the environment. Research has consistently demonstrated that characteristics of the office environment can have a significant effect on behavior, perceptions, and productivity of workers.[4]

At the time, Chris Hughes, my old boss from the fire department, was the city manager. I asked Chris if I should worry about someone from the city council visiting the dispatch center one night and finding the dispatchers crocheting. He said, "I'm not worried; show them the stats and data. The activities are imperative to their mental health and improve performance. Let your work speak for itself."

Together, we brought a new culture paradigm to government. An unexpected benefit was that improving workplace culture in dispatch brought the sworn and civilian sides of the house together. Sworn officers, whose motto was "if you aren't sworn, you aren't shit" now showed gratitude and respect for the dispatchers.

The dispatchers were proud of their work in the new dispatch center and attrition, which had been high before the overhaul, dissipated. As we physically changed the environment and self-image, the culture and attitudes changed dramatically.

---

4   Altman, I., & Lett, E. E., The ecology of interpersonal relationships: A classification system and conceptual model, in J.E. McGrathe (Ed.), Social and psychological factors in stress, (New York: Holt Rinehart 1969).

We had "SEE CLEARLY" outcomes.

SEE CLEARLY

When the leader commits to *wearing* his sunglasses and embracing authenticity, ten additional benefits are realized:

- **S**afety
- **E**mpathy
- **E**mpowerment
- **C**ollective Leadership
- **L**everage Adversity
- **E**mbrace Risk
- **A**ccountability
- **R**ise Above Challenges
- **L**ove Your Purpose
- **Y**our Wins Matter

An authentic organization that has all these elements will be able to push the boundaries, take on new ambitions, and have a successful team.

SAFETY

Authenticity and safety go hand in hand. When people feel that their basic needs are being met, they feel safe. An authentic environment is free from ridicule and judgment. Employees know they can enter the workplace, walk to their desks, and feel welcome. The second level of Maslow's hierarchy of needs in the workplace[5], safety (following basic physiological needs), is satisfied. Safety is the first benefit to come to light in an authentic environment; all the other benefits follow. Just as with Maslow's pyramid, the employee satisfied at the safety level can move on to the next need. Safety also encompasses the idea that employees feel comfortable speaking up about their needs or weaknesses, as discussed in the previous chapter.

EMPATHY

In an authentic environment, mutual respect develops as individuals with complementary skills are valued for the differences they bring to the team. Individuals feel safe expressing a contrarian perspective while conveying their displeasure from a position of mutual understanding.

The leader who lacks empathy is one who is quick to say a person should be fired, quick to dismiss a way of looking at a situation in a way that's different than his. Authentic organizations don't have that level of judgment. Empathy means pausing and then asking why the other person is

---

5   William Kremer and Claudia Hammond, "Abraham Maslow and the pyramid that beguiled business," BBC World Service (September 2013) https://www.bbc.com/news/magazine-23902918

advocating for a particular resolution. Empathy sounds like, "Tell me more about how that solution has worked in the past. Why do you feel the solution I offered is a bad idea?" True empathy is seeking clarity instead of immediate dismissal.

EMPOWERMENT

In an authentic organization, employees feel empowered to have a voice, to make an impact, and to help steer the course of the team or organization. This doesn't mean that you disband the hierarchy or eliminate oversight; it simply means that helicopter parenting doesn't need to be applied to every situation in the workplace. Giving employees an opportunity to be an active part of the creative process and the freedom to be responsible for their own outcomes will help create a feeling of empowerment. Empowered employees will be more engaged, more attached, and more effective in their tasks.

Safety, Empathy, and Empowerment Working Together

When I met Ethan, he was a twenty-three-year-old college graduate working as a customer service representative in another city department. Ethan's reputation as a young gun preceded him; I'd heard from his department's manager that he was an up-and-comer to keep an eye out for. I was a department director at the time and Ethan reached out and asked if he could volunteer on Fridays—his day off—in my department. Always the go-getter, I took Ethan on as an intern working directly for me. I told him that my goal would be to expose him to as many different areas as possible but that we also really needed an intern to pitch in with some of the less desirable duties. He took on everything we tossed his way without any complaint, exceeding our expectations. If we asked him to handle filing, he would create new filing systems and pursued technologies to help simplify and streamline the process. He always asked, "Isn't there a better way to do this?" Some may have been intimidated, but for me, it was an opportunity to learn a lot from someone who represented a generation of ingenuity, out-of-the-box thinking, and an understanding of public sector purpose. Later, when I had the opportunity, I hired Ethan as my assistant.

Although we had already worked together, I asked Ethan about his interests and professional ambitions when he took on the role as my assistant. I wanted to keep him involved in projects that stimulated and fulfilled him. Ethan was positive, enthusiastic, full of energy, and confident. He anticipated my needs. He set up systems and structures to compensate for my deficits, challenges, and memory problems. He knew more than others about my injury and knew the perfect balance between friendly banter and respectful support. Then one day about nine months into the job, he walked into my office and said,

"I feel like I should get a different job." The first question that came to mind was to ask him why. His enthusiasm for the job told me he liked the work he was doing and our working relationship.

Ethan said, "Because I feel like you don't invest in me." I felt like someone had punched me in the stomach. I prided myself on being a good manager who invested in my team, and Ethan's comment couldn't have been farther from the intention of my actions. I could see that he was hurt.

In an even voice with true curiosity, I said, "Ethan, what do you mean? In the last nine months, I've sent you to six conferences. I've sent you to get new certifications. I've had you attend countless meetings with me so that you could see some of the major discussions and policy issues that I deal with, exposure that nobody else in your position has access to. What do you mean you feel like I'm not investing in you?"

Ethan agreed that I'd done those things but added that he felt like he didn't have a voice. I could have expressed anger or frustration and called him an ungrateful millennial who's not worthy of the position. Instead, I reached for empathy. I asked him what it would look like if he had a voice in this organization, what it would look like for him to come to work and feel like I was invested in him.

He shared what having a voice meant to him. He wanted to be consulted after meetings we attended. He wanted to be debriefed. He wanted an opportunity to influence the decisions I was making. It was important to me that he felt fulfilled each day at work. More importantly, I wanted to be sure someone who was working so hard on my behalf had their needs met. And, almost without exception, his ideas were much better than mine!

Because I had created an authentic environment, Ethan felt safe to come to me and have this conversation. Instead of dismissing him, I wanted to learn what I could do to make his environment better.

When Ethan came into my office and said he felt he didn't have a voice, I paused. While my initial gut reaction may have been that he had a crazy, ridiculous, and ungrateful point of view, I put myself in Ethan's shoes and wanted to understand why he was advocating for the resolution he wanted. I wanted to know what in his life brought him to my office that day. Rather than quickly concluding that I didn't agree with what he was saying, I wanted to see the situation from his point of view.

I saw a professional who brought competency and enthusiasm to the workplace and as the leader, it was my responsibility to address the one thing that made him feel defeated. After our conversation, we implemented some of Ethan's ideas, and he began to see results. While he had felt marginalized before, he was now more empowered. Within eighteen months of working for me, Ethan was promoted again, and he's been promoted twice since by others for his continued stellar performance and willingness to bring a new and fresh perspective to traditional government.

COLLECTIVE LEADERSHIP

Collective leadership means that leadership isn't left to the highest level of the organization and that we all have the responsibility to step up and lead at different parts of the journey. Many leaders are great at bringing in various levels of the organization into the decision-making process when appropriate. In doing so, employees feel like they have a vested stake in the future of the company and decisions are made with more immediacy and less red tape.

Collective Leadership Blunder

When employees are left on the sidelines, the results can be disastrous. One of the biggest mistakes I made in my career was overlooking the importance of bringing the front-line operators into a major operational decision.

I had heard from my dispatchers that the police records

channel—a radio channel used by officers to receive information they need while on a call, such as warrant information or vehicle registration information—was best suited to be managed by employees from the records division (non-dispatchers). Some dispatchers argued that their phone lines and primary radio frequencies needed more hands and freeing up the records channel dispatcher and replacing her with a records specialist (who normally manages Public Records Act requests and filing responsibilities) would be a better match.

This was a great idea, or so I thought. I put together a fancy report and briefed the entire department on the date of transition and the wonderful efficiencies that would be realized as a result of this transfer. Reluctantly, but being good soldiers, the records specialists (none of whom had any radio channel experience) took a few brief training classes and assumed their role on the police records channel on day one.

By the end of the day, I had created a major labor relations crisis. Officers were upset by delays and training issues, dispatchers were angry with a poorly executed roll-out, and the records specialists justifiably felt like I had thrown them to the wolves. Above all, the records personnel rightfully pointed out that I had never included them in the project development process. They had to hear information from the rumor mill or from other dispatchers, and although I invested a lot of time in their operation, I spent no time vetting this project with them. The only thing that saved my career was an immediate email I sent to the organization taking full responsibility for the failure of the project and terminating it immediately. We decided to keep dispatchers on all radio channels, and we kept the records specialists as the behind-the-scenes experts that could continue to support the dispatch team without the pressure of a headset and radio channel.

Leaders must create environments where the team feels they can engage and help take the organization forward. Nobody should be left behind in process improvements.

LEVERAGE ADVERSITY

Human beings have a natural tendency to run from challenges and adversity. Why would we embrace that which is difficult, challenging, or a loss? In dealing with my own challenges, I realized that part of that response comes from shame and embarrassment; we don't want to be seen as having weaknesses. I learned, however, that great power comes from looking the situation in the face and hitting it head on. When we define the challenge, we begin to control it. Leveraging adversity is about actively creating value even when the obstacles ahead would sink most people.

Run into the Florescent Light

My visual impairment was a source of insecurity before, but today I've changed it into a source of strength by taking control of that which held me back. Wearing my sunglasses has brought many benefits: the energy I used for pain management is now used for work, people lower their defenses around me, and I relate better to my team because I have a daily reminder that shows I'm compensating for a gap that I know I have. The team, in turn, knows they can identify their gaps and compensate for them rather than run from them. We wear our sunglasses and run into a fluorescent-lit room.

So too should a team stop to think about the lessons and resilience that can come from a great organizational challenge. Many of the companies I've worked with recently have called me in after enduring layoffs. The layoff process not only impacts those who lost their jobs, but also those remaining who feel anxious and unsettled because their network has been reconfigured. Some employees leave their jobs, but those who look at the situation and try to figure out ways to find clarity and use it to strengthen their team have gone on to promote in the organization and spread their ability to make an impact. There are often opportunities to obtain a benefit from a challenge that never would have been achieved without the adversity.

EMBRACE RISK

While embracing risk may come easily in a startup, it's difficult in well-established organizations, especially in the public sector. When faced with change, it's easy to think "We've always done it this way. Why should we change?"

In an authentic environment, people are more willing to embrace risk because they know they won't be viewed as a failure. They understand that it's okay to fail and build compensatory techniques to fill gaps. People who don't work in an authentic environment won't ever try something that might lead to failure, which actually stunts their personal growth and the organization's growth. When we fail, we're not a failure, it's just an opportunity to find the gap, fill it, and try again.

Social Media Anxiety

Rapid change in technology and modern communication requires that organizations adopt a willingness to evolve quickly. I worked in the economic development office for the city of Ontario when social media started growing in popularity in the public sector (the private sector was years ahead of public sector social media integration). The organization was against social media because the risk of releasing the wrong information before it had been approved or missing a constituent's comment was too great. While other communities adopted and integrated social media, our response was an emphatic "No." We were risk-averse. Personally, I was afraid my bosses would frown upon any entrée to social media, and if a problem erupted, I would be responsible. I should have asked, "What's the worst possible thing that could happen?" and not been so consumed by my insecurity.

Our aversion to risk kept us from connecting with our entire customer base. The city of Ontario prided itself on being business-friendly and business-focused. For decades we had made it easy for companies to set up their corporate headquarters in Ontario. Our stakeholders, current and potential, were using social media to connect and we were absent from the scene. When I became the business operations director, the millennials on my team begged me to transition to social media. I toed the organizational line and said, "No. It's too risky. What if unapproved messages are released? Government doesn't need to be on the cutting edge." In hindsight, what I was telling them was, "I don't understand social media. I'm totally intimidated. I'm nervous and scared to use it." For at least a year, they knocked on my door every day and tried different arguments to change my mind.

Tanya, one of the economic development specialists, gave me a different perspective to consider. She said we weren't going to be able to maintain our competitive advantage over other cities by solely depending on our reputation to attract new business. We had to reach the decision makers where they were assembling: social media. She told me that by being absent on social media, we were neglecting our target market and not showing up to the party. While that party used to be solely networking events and state of the city, deals were now being explored via social media and we had a small window to arrive or we would never be invited again. She also pointed out that much smaller neighboring cities were growing a large following, and she questioned whether or not some of their recent business attraction success and positive media praise had been a fallout from Ontario's lack of a social media presence. I listened and absorbed her observations and (finally) acquiesced. Within a few days of creating our Facebook profile, we had an outpouring of positive support and comments, including one that said, "Thank you for finally getting with the program!" I felt guilty for having held the organization back for so long because I wasn't willing to embrace a risk that was small compared to the benefits. I also ignored the expertise of my team and let my own insecurities dominate my decision making—never a winning strategy.

The leader who resists risk needs to stop and think about why he's so resistant. He should conduct some self-inquiry and ask himself:

- Am I resisting change because I am uncomfortable with this?
- Do I need more information to feel more comfortable and understand this change?
- Is this because I'm insecure that my staff or people around me know more about this issue than I do?
- Am I unfairly putting my own personal beliefs on the organization to the detriment of my team and the organization?
- What can I do so that I can learn more about this change or risk and make a decision that's in the best interest of my organization, and not just looking out for my own need to feel comfortable?

ACCOUNTABILITY

A shift occurs in authentic organizations. New managers think their job is to hold employees accountable. In authentic organizations that have gone through this process, employees also take on the responsibility for accountability. When the other benefits fall in line—the environment feels safe, leaders and staff demonstrate empathy, and employees feel empowered and engaged—employees begin to hold themselves and each other accountable.

When I took over the dispatch center at the police department, I inherited a troublesome situation. While dispatch performance was stellar, absenteeism, attrition, and reports of misconduct were high. Many believed the center needed disciplinary action along with strong change management. When I conducted one-on-one intake sessions with every employee, one name continued to surface. We'll call her Pamela.

Pamela was a tenured twenty-plus year dispatch supervisor. Many employees shared stories of intimidation and a failure to properly supervise with me. I brought in additional resources for Pamela, but her behavior and attitude didn't change. Ultimately, after getting wind of some unacceptable situations that broke numerous policies, I had to terminate Pamela. She appealed the disciplinary action at every level available, and in each scenario, all charges I had brought against her were upheld. As the leader, I had to hold her accountable for her actions, and I had to be accountable as the leader for the rest of the team.

I tackled other personnel cases as well. Each time someone crossed the line, I approached them with the same discussion. "We've spent eighteen months rebuilding the dispatch center," I'd say to them. "You have tremendous skill and competency and know this job inside and out, but your conduct—the way in which you deal with others—is not acceptable. I will not make the choice for you. I will give you the freedom to choose whether or not you are going to get on this train and proceed toward a customer-focused environment or if you are going to choose to continue to act and behave the same way. Either way, there will be consequences to whichever path you choose. The choice is yours." I conveyed in each scenario that if their behavior improved, they would have a strong role in helping others and being a core part of taking the team to the next level. I needed each employee's skill and experience on the team, but it wouldn't be at the expense of team solidarity.

Almost without exception, when I gave the employee the choice of their future path, they got with the program. Rapid improvement followed, and most team members engaged by making recommendations for improvements, challenging management appropriately, and many were promoted and became mentors for other rookie dispatchers.

A curious, extraordinary change also happened in the overall culture. Throughout the entire dispatch center, instead of management having to open cases and conduct personnel investigations, dispatchers were holding each other accountable. There was a new sense of ownership over the operation. The dispatchers didn't want the environment to return to the disciplinary state it had been in when I took over the position. They wanted to perform at an even higher level, as a cohesive team.

RISE ABOVE CHALLENGES

In an authentic environment where leaders and staff are self-aware, adversity becomes a learning tool that can usually be leveraged. The manager leads the team to face obstacles head-on rather than run away and to identify gaps and build compensatory techniques. Some challenges, however, can't be leveraged. Sometimes the team has to figure out how to steer around it, which may mean pivoting from the challenge, putting it in its place, not letting it dominate the landscape. It's the leader's responsibility to decide to go a different way and not waste any more time or energy on the adversity. A good leader will be able to assess when a challenge can be leveraged as an advantage or when it needs to be navigated around.

LOVE YOUR PURPOSE

Leaders and managers have to make sure that each of the team members are connected to the purpose of the work that we're doing. As Simon Sinek says, "we have to take time to explain the why."

Loving your purpose means deeply connecting with the *why* of the organization. In an authentic environment, the leader invests time with the staff to help them connect to their own purpose and that of the organization.

Veterans vs. Rookies

I often heard from veteran dispatchers that "rookies just don't understand our job. They don't appreciate and respect what the veteran dispatchers have been through." As part of the eighteen-month overhaul of the dispatch department, I brought together veteran dispatchers and asked them for help. I asked the veteran group to tell me why they had originally signed up to work as dispatchers.

My goal was two-fold: I wanted the veterans, some of whom were suffering from burnout after a decorated career, to reconnect with their purpose; and I wanted to develop a "why" statement for other dispatchers to embrace, inspired by the work of Simon Sinek. The carefully worded "why" statement we created together was, "We chose a profession that's in the business of helping others."

Each word had a purpose:

- *Chose* reflected that being a dispatcher was an active choice; no one had to stay if they didn't want to.

- *Profession* reflected the pride of what we did; it was more than a job.
- *Business* reflected the formal, structured environment where everyone had a role in the operation's success.
- *Helping* meant that every single day should be focused on service.

The finishing touch of the dispatch center environment overhaul (described earlier in this chapter) was placing that statement on a plaque, along with the badges from the respective public safety agencies we served, and hanging it just above the key pad to open the door to the dispatch room. Every employee coming in understood exactly what the dispatch profession embodied. Entering the dispatch center meant entering an environment connected to the personal and organizational purpose and to each other. Veteran staff were reminded of why they're in this profession. The "why" statement created a commonality between the rookie and veteran dispatchers.

New leaders have to take the time to explain the purpose behind the changes they're making. Employees who hear a boss say, "My way or the highway," are likely to take to the road. Attrition in the dispatch center dropped to zero after the eighteen-month overhaul process—not because of the project itself, but because each person understood their role in our division's success.

YOUR WINS MATTER

Your wins matter. Authentic organizations don't wait until the big goal is reached to celebrate; they celebrate the journey and the steps along the way. They pause to appreciate and celebrate the forward progress. Leaders have to look for opportunities to recognize the team and celebrate those small victories. Recognizing incremental improvements motivates the staff. It's important to have long-term goals, but the victory isn't limited to the end-of-the-year sales goal.

Lights, Sirens, Action!

Early in my career in public service, I worked as a dispatcher in a much smaller and slower agency than Ontario. The 911 calls received were usually medical aid calls, domestic violence calls, fight calls, and lots of calls about barking dogs. Every once in a while, we had a "big city" night. On one such night, a call came in reporting a fire alarm at a large building. Standard call. I dispatched the fire department and one officer per protocol. A few minutes after the officer arrived on scene, a firefighter called me in dispatch on the officer's radio. The firefighter told me that the officer was unconscious, and the fire personnel had two subjects detained that they assumed were arson suspects—that's not a situation in the handbook! Not knowing what had happened, I rolled additional police units with lights and sirens to aid our officer. Things accelerated quickly. At about the time it was determined that the officer was suffering from a cardiac medical condition (and hadn't been assaulted by the arson suspects as I had deduced), another 911 call came in regarding a fight between ten to fifteen subjects outside a fitness facility. I sent a few officers and within minutes of their arrival, they were calling for additional officers to respond with lights and sirens and the dreaded "officer needs assistance" call went out over the radio, followed by reports of pepper spray, Taser usage, and baton strikes deployed. I was the only dispatcher on duty, and I was still managing the aftermath of the arson situation while simultaneously handling the primary dispatch radio, coordinating the activation and response of officers from two neighboring departments, handling incoming calls, and doing my best to make department top brass notifications. We were slammed for the next three to four hours, handling all sorts of odd calls for service—clearly a full moon. My shift ended, and while we were all exhausted, we felt a strong sense of accomplishment and unity.

The next day I came to work, there was a large box with my name on it near the dispatch console. Attached was a note from the department's saltiest, albeit one of the most tenured and squared away officers that had worked our previous shift. He was the kind of guy that greeted you with sarcasm and disdain, but when things went south, he was the best in the business. On the card he wrote, "Enjoy the cookies, outstanding work last night, thanks for taking care of us." I was proud of our team the night before, but nothing matched the feeling I had receiving that card. It was a small, low-cost gesture that gave big returns and reinforced my love of the profession and my fellow officers. I felt like I had value and purpose, and I was humbled that the officer took the time to recognize this team win.

Wins aren't limited to successfully managing dramatic events. Learning and growth are also cause for celebration. New managers should identify metrics they're able to celebrate with frequency. The team needs to know that what they're doing is making a difference; regular recognition and celebration create connection. What's more, if the big goal isn't reached, celebrating smaller wins ensures the team won't feel like the progress along the way was a wasted effort.

PUTTING IT ALL TOGETHER

New leaders and recently-promoted managers have to look at the "SEE CLEARLY" mnemonic. "SEE CLEARLY" and authentic organizations are two sides of the same coin. Authentic organizations enable these outcomes, and these outcomes reinforce authenticity. Leaders must think about what they can do to actively affect these outcomes and can ask themselves:

- Is there collective leadership in my organization? In my team?
- Does my team embrace risk?
- Does my team leverage adversity?

The most effective, highly efficient, and successful divisions or teams have all of these elements. When a team is missing one of the beneficial outcomes, it's time well invested to consider why it's missing and what can be done to bring it forth.

CHAPTER 7

———

LEARN TO LEAN

Rehabilitation taught me to lean on others, heavily and often, when needed. I didn't have all the answers before my injury and certainly never admitted to it. After the injury and through rehabilitation, I learned that even my heroes have blind spots and the need to seek answers from others.

Brain injuries don't discriminate. I attended brain injury rehabilitation school with a dentist, a lawyer, a psychologist, and an author. They were perhaps the best in their fields before their injuries—the person that everyone went to for the answers—and in an instant, everything changed. They no longer had those same answers, those skills. A big part of rehabilitation is learning when and how to lean on others. Once I became good at leaning on people, I understood that leaning is not weakness.

Leaning on people is the strength of having the confidence to say, "I am okay and not less of a man or a woman if I lean on others. I grow when I learn from others. I become better at being who I am by leaning on others. I become more focused and waste less time and energy if I lean on others."

THUNDER BUDDY

New leaders are wise to seek out one or two people who they trust completely to support them and give honest feedback. As a leader climbs the organization's ladder, he learns he won't receive approval from everyone. He often has to make tough decisions that are good for the organization but don't please everyone on the team. The staff will openly criticize the leader's decisions. I once received an employee survey that said, "I can't believe he's a motivational speaker, there's nothing motivational about him. He's the un-motivational speaker." Prior to my brain injury, this would have thrown me off the rails. But with a much stronger sense of self, I use these opportunities to embrace the following quote by Epictetus:

> If anyone tells you that a certain person speaks ill of you, do not make excuses about what is said of you but answer, 'He was ignorant of my other faults, else he would not have mentioned these alone.'

New leaders have to thicken their skin and find a few people who will keep them centered and balanced. This support circle may include a spouse and friends from outside work but should also include one or two confidantes within the organization. They need a thunder buddy.

I looked to the city manager. I looked to the executives. I tried to study and learn as much as I could from everyone who was above me. Then I met Darryl Polk. Darryl and I naturally connected when I was working in the fire department, and Darryl was a dispatch supervisor. We had crossed paths in emergency management planning, and we discovered we enjoyed many of the same things. I sought counsel from Darryl, and slowly we became thunder buddies, even (and especially) when I later landed the job overseeing the dispatch center and there was a level of management between our two positions.

Darryl was the guy who could tell me when I was off my rocker, when I had gone too far, and when the troops were feeling that their leader was out of touch with them. He was willing to give me honest, hard feedback because he knew that I wanted what was best for the organization and our peers. Without Darryl's trust and input, I would have been quite alone and not nearly as successful. Today, Darryl and I work for different cities, but we've maintained our partnership, regularly calling upon each other for brutally honest feedback. I'd like to think that my candid advice to Darryl played a small role in his rapid ascension through the ranks where he currently resides as the chief technology officer for a large Southern California city.

NOT A MENTOR

A thunder buddy is not a mentor. The mentor-mentee relationship is one way, with the mentor providing guidance to the mentee. Mentors don't seek support from their mentees and rarely will they lean on them. The mentee typically seeks out the mentor. I've reached out to potential mentors and said, "Can we meet for coffee or a quick lunch?" Rarely does the mentor say, "Today, I'm going to find someone who would benefit from my advice."

The thunder buddy relationship may be initiated by one party; it takes one party to lean in and create that connection. After the initial connection, the thunder buddy is a partner, and there is a mutual two-way exchange.

There are lots of thunder buddies in history: Penn and Teller, Laurel and Hardy. I heard the term in the movie, *Ted,* where Mark Wahlberg's character and a stuffed bear are thunder buddies. They're successful because they're so different and willing to bring different perspectives and approaches to the table; they share similar values yet complementary skills. They fill each other's gaps. Teller doesn't speak, but he contributes to Penn & Teller's performances. They're good because they're so different.

INVESTED IN THE OTHER'S SUCCESS

Thunder buddies look beyond what the relationship does for them and provide a different paradigm and perspective to each other. A conversation between thunder buddies may sound like two people who don't agree on anything. It's really a process of discerning and mining and making sure that situations are looked at from different angles. Thunder buddies challenge each other with respect and reach better outcomes.

Darryl and I are one hundred percent invested in the other's success. I'm willing and able to tell him things that nobody else will say about things he should be doing differently or different approaches he should take. The qualities of a thunder buddy are many:

- They truly love and care about each other and are invested in each other's success.
- They enable each other to be confident because they support each other.
- There is synergy and authenticity that allows each to be tensile.
- They're brutally honest and willing to share alternate viewpoints to avoid group think and myopic thinking.

- "The whole is greater than the sum of its parts."—Aristotle

LISTEN TO YOUR THUNDER BUDDY

Darryl and I were in a meeting with my dispatch management team. We were talking about the relationship between the dispatch center and fire helicopter services. I said "Well, we don't have to worry about this because there will never be a fire helicopter in that city." Darryl said, "Well no, Jacob, that city will be getting a fire helicopter soon." We went back and forth. I insisted that a small city didn't have the money or resources to get a fire helicopter, and Darryl insisted it would happen. In the end, I placed a bet with Darryl that if that other city got a fire helicopter, I would take the entire management team to dinner. Darryl counseled me not to place a bet, but I went ahead anyway. The next morning, the front-page headline of the local newspaper said "City Secures New Fire Helicopter."

When I talked to Darryl about it later, he said, "You really should never bet against your staff." It had nothing to do with being wrong or right; it was that I had been arrogant to insist on my point of view against my own team. Darryl was right, and I appreciated his honesty. Thanks to my thunder buddy, I left that experience $500 poorer but with a tremendous wealth of insight about the damage

MY THUNDER BUDDY, BY DARRYL POLK

Jacob and I have worked together in multiple capacities and relationships, and over the years, we became close, trusted friends. I first met Jacob in summer of 2005, when he started as a disaster preparedness analyst for the Ontario Fire Department. I was working as a fire dispatch shift supervisor at the time, and we found that we shared time working the 911 boards. Jacob was unassuming and easy to talk with, which were historically not hallmarks of disaster preparedness staff. We quickly became friends and found that our relationship provided an important new resource for both of us. Having a friend who works in the same field, but not in the same environment, gave us both a sounding board to seek advice, test ideas, and vent our frustrations. This ability to "download" became a centerpiece of our relationship over time.

It's why we partner up with spouses and why we have "best friends." It's about having someone who you trust implicitly and unreservedly to tell you not what you want to hear, but what you need to hear. Finding someone like this is not easy and maintaining it is even more difficult. It means really letting your guard down and truly trusting that, no matter what is said, your thunder buddy always has your best interests at heart.

As we move through different stages of our careers, we encounter progressive levels of leadership. At first, leadership simply means having the self-direction and discipline to make the right decisions about your own actions. How to not just do what you're told, but to accomplish what is expected of you. As things progress, we find ourselves making decisions for others, continually broadening the scope and impact of our decisions as we move up in the organization. The people who work for us, with us, and who we work for expect certainty. The problem is our decisions impact everyone around us, making it difficult to confide in someone about self-doubt. This is where leaders often trip up—making decisions in a vacuum without the benefit of an outside perspective.

Jacob and I both recognized the value of our relationship early on. We understood what it was to be Thunder Buddies and found that the more trust we placed in each other, the more trust we earned. It meant being extremely vulnerable with each other, which is not something often discussed about leadership. Facing and embracing the gaps in our abilities and our shortcomings as leaders allowed us to become more authentic not only with each other, but with those around us. Just being able to talk through doubt early and thoroughly meant it couldn't develop into fears and insecurities. It made us more confident in our decisions and made us both better leaders, which proved out as both our careers continued to advance.

that I could do as an arrogant leader. Without my thunder buddy, I don't know that I would ever have understood that lesson. I didn't see the big picture. I didn't understand how I was being perceived. My thunder buddy helped me see all those things and connect all those dots. I don't think anyone else in that room would have provided that follow-up except for Darryl.

Leaders without an authentic thunder buddy relationship risk becoming limited leaders. They may respond with ambition to every challenge. They don't lean on or trust others. They don't know how to listen. Respect is replaced with competition and self-righteousness. Their entire life becomes a struggle for power.

LEAN ON YOUR TEAM

New leaders are often promoted because of something they've done on their own, but their strengths may lie in putting together a powerful team of people with diverse backgrounds and perspectives united under a desire and a passion for the mission and task at hand. When a leader leverages everyone's strengths and backgrounds, he'll be able to accomplish things no one thought was possible.

So much of my experience has been about understanding my own limitations. I have a critical need to fill the gaps and weaknesses in myself by leaning on others and building a powerful team.

Ontario, California, is a fifty-square mile city, and right in the middle of the city is the Ontario International Airport. The airport has been in operation since the 1920s. In the 1960s, it became the diversion airport for the Los Angeles International Airport. Whenever fog or other conditions made landing at LAX impossible, planes were diverted to Ontario International Airport. In 1967, the leaders of Ontario handed over operations of the airport to LAX. In 1985, the city of Los Angeles asked for full ownership, and the leaders of Ontario gave Los Angeles the keys—perhaps they were star struck. All was well and good until the city of Ontario began to grow and "compete" with Los Angeles for business. Ontario's success as a business hub was a direct threat to Los Angeles's economic prosperity.

To keep businesses in Los Angeles, the powers that be directed the majority of flights to LAX, which limited the approach to regional air service that is key to a successful transportation network. Ontario's number of departures and passenger traffic declined rapidly.

In fact, by 2010, the passenger traffic had dwindled to less than fifty percent of what it had been in previous decades. The Ontario City Council decided it was time to take back local control of the airport before it was driven into the ground.

In 2012, City Manager Chris Hughes called me into his office. Despite repeated demands and attempted negotiations, Los Angeles refused to cede control back to Ontario. The city manager said, "Jacob. I want to show you something." He took a blue yard sign out from behind his door that read, "Set Ontario Free." "This," he said, "is going to be the slogan for our new campaign to take back ownership of the airport. And you, Jacob, are going to take point on the marketing campaign."

My specific job, as Chris explained, was to get resolutions passed by cities throughout Southern California in support of the transfer of Ontario International Airport from the city of LA to Ontario, California. Chris believed this undertaking, if successful, would convince Los Angeles that the greater Southern California region needed a revitalization of the aviation network, and its best chance was an Ontario Airport turnaround. I was put in charge of the initiative with support and guidance from a gifted city consultant who had developed the campaign branding with the city manager and former city manager Greg Devereaux.

In government, there's an unwritten rule that you don't meddle in another city's business. I saw two immediate problems. First, I had a hard time understanding why another city council would pass a resolution against Los Angeles and in favor of Ontario's desire to regain control over Ontario International Airport. Second, I had no experience running public policy education campaigns or seeking city council resolutions. I said to Chris, "OK, we'll figure this out."

I knew this project represented a major gap in my skills. But I also knew that Chris saw something in my abilities to contribute to this goal. I would need a team with the skills and abilities that filled my own gaps and weaknesses.

I pulled people from the fire department, the police department, IT, and the economic development agency. I put together a team of a dozen experts with experience in media relations, website design, social media, SEO, and business management.

At our first meeting, I explained our mission, and we brainstormed ways to draw attention to the Set Ontario Free campaign. We developed a list of close to one hundred concepts, including a TV commercial, a social media competition, giveaways at local community and sporting events, and public service announcements. Everything was fair game, everything was put up on the white board, and the focus was educating the public and building a network of informed community members.

I asked Chris to come to our second meeting, so I could explain our plans. He was worried about confidentiality and said he'd assigned the task to me alone. I explained that I didn't have all the answers. We gave a thirty-minute presentation of the things we planned to do. No one person had 360-degree experience with a marketing campaign or public policy initiative, but they all brought their individual strengths and added value to the overall mission. The sum of the parts was once again greater than the whole. Chris was impressed and gave us the green light to proceed with many of our proposed initiatives.

Over the next several years, we received 133 formal resolutions and official agency letters in support of local control of the Ontario International Airport, an amazing accomplishment carried out as a result of a clear vision from the city council and the willingness of city management to let a group of diverse employees try some untested tactics to engage the community. In the fall of 2015, with public pressure reaching a boiling point and negotiations in full throttle, the Ontario City Council was successful in working with Los Angeles to affect a transfer, and on November 1st, 2016, the Ontario International Airport was finally transferred back under local control. It was an unprecedented educational campaign. Today, the airport is bustling with new domestic and international flights, new airlines, refurbished terminals, and passenger traffic this year is the highest it's been over the last decade.

CONCLUSION

Momentum plays a significant role in all of our lives. What we experience as children carries over into adulthood, forming a foundation for how we see the world. The victories and defeats of our youth become the prism in which we see our potential as adults. Our earliest exposures can shape how we view the landscape, casting a shadow or light that we often fail to recognize in our future selves.

Growing up, my family made honoring public service a cornerstone of our values. If a group of policemen or firemen was eating at a restaurant where we were dining, my father always paid the bill. He would summon the waiter, ask for the bill, and instruct the waiter not to share his identity. He respected the risk the police and fire professionals took every day they went to work and wanted to show his appreciation in some small way, without any recognition in return. It was a selfless instinct to honor the contributions others have made for our benefit. It is perhaps his respect for public servants that instilled a desire in me to become one.

At eighteen, it seemed that door was wide open for me, until that second semester of my freshman year at the Shattuck BART station, when my world changed overnight. After my brain injury, I didn't know who I was or what I would become. I felt unprepared and anxious about my future. With the help of my family, friends, many committed doctors, healthcare providers, and experts, I slowly got back on my feet and entered my chosen profession.

Sitting on the edge of my murphy bed in my small studio apartment just a half mile from my rehabilitation facility, I dreamt of being able to use the lessons I was learning about navigating overnight change to one day provide some usefulness to others. My days felt empty, and some nights, I would jump in my car and drive up and down Southern California's Pacific Coast Highway just to pass the time and make it through one more night. I focused on the long play—the knowledge that someday there would be value in these challenges.

Little did I know at the time how much my experience following my brain injury would mirror what I would encounter in my future professional life. Whenever I transitioned to a new leadership position or took on a challenging project, I felt the same sense of chaos—the confusion, the lack of self-awareness, and the loss of identity. I had no idea at the time how helpful the tools for dealing with a brain injury would be in the workplace or how universal the need for these tools is.

THREE SIMPLE STEPS

When confronted with managing chaos and change in the workplace, new managers often don't know what to do or where to begin. Leaders can follow the steps I learned in brain school:

1. Identify the gaps
2. Develop compensatory techniques
3. Implement those techniques

Self-awareness and emotional intelligence are the keys to creating a high-functioning environment that embraces cognitive diversity. An authentic workplace brings positive benefits and outcomes to employees and leaders alike. Remember SEE CLEARLY:

- **S**afety
- **E**mpathy
- **E**mpowerment
- **C**ollective Leadership

- Leverage Adversity
- Embrace Risk
- Accountability
- Rise Above Challenges
- Love Your Purpose
- Your Wins Matter

I wrote this book to share the lessons I learned and help provide insight to anyone facing the self-doubt and apprehension of a new leadership position. My medical journey was worth every step because it prepared me to make a positive impact on my teams, my workplace, and my life.

If someone had told me brain injury would teach me how to be successful in business, I wouldn't have believed them. Yet, through brain injury and my subsequent rehabilitation, I learned the power of restraint in assessing problems before trying to solve them. I learned the power of logically building compensatory techniques to find solutions. I learned to speak with candor without shying away from vulnerability and to encourage others I worked with to do so as well. I learned how much energy is recaptured from jettisoning false pretenses and shielding our weaknesses.

We all have challenges and issues, which means we also have insecurities about how we deal with them. How much better would the workplace be if we got over seeing these as unsolvable barriers and instead invested our collective energy into creating compensatory strategies that not only solve immediate problems, but also build trust toward overcoming future obstacles.

The most powerful teams I've ever been a part of—the Set Ontario Free airport team, the emergency operations center team, the toilet response team, the homeless services emergency management team, and teams in my current job—are the ones that learned to value and embrace the diversity of their members. They understand that differences in thought and approach can be an unparalleled strength if the team has the maturity to handle conflict constructively. On these teams, I wasn't shunned for having a brain injury. I was valued for having a methodical approach that often kept the team from making rash decisions or taking ill-considered actions. Teams that can harness the power of conflict and make it a constructive part of daily activities find themselves able to repeat success. They quickly find that not every disagreement is a fight, and not every problem is a crisis. Challenges become building blocks toward future aspirations.

FACING ADVERSITY BUILDS INNER STRENGTH

I dedicated this book to Brianne Schwantes. Brianne was born with osteogenesis imperfecta, or brittle bone disease. When she was born, doctors told her parents she would never walk alone or be able to live alone; she went on to do both.

I met Brianne Schwantes in 1996 when we were recognized with a National Caring Award in Washington, DC. We were both sixteen. Brianne was being celebrated for her volunteerism, service, and advocacy work and the countless people she'd influenced despite having had over one hundred surgeries since birth and being hospitalized on a regular basis. She testified before Congress seven times (starting at age eight) to seek more funding for the National Institutes of Health, created international networks for children with rare diseases, aided flood victims in Iowa, served as a mentor and champion for kids with HIV and other chronic diseases, and was a gifted public speaker focused on helping teens overcome challenges. She's been interviewed by Oprah, recognized publicly by two presidents, and received a personal letter written from then-president Bill Clinton.

Before arriving in DC to accept the award, I had read Brianne's bio, and besides feeling radically unworthy compared to her humanitarian impacts, I was also quite nervous to meet her in person—both starstruck and awkward about how I would respond to her physical limitations. Would shaking her hand break a bone? Would giving her a hug put her back in the hospital? What were the rules? Our first meeting was an unexpected one as I waited for an elevator in the DC hotel. She walked out of the elevator and before I could say a word, she said, "Oh my god! it's *the* Jacob Green. You're as good looking as your photo, but what's up with that ridiculous haircut! Didn't flat tops go out of style in the 80s?" I busted up laughing, and she instantly broke down any barriers I had erected between us.

We became close friends over the years. When I suffered my brain injury three years after our first meeting, Brianne was instrumental in getting me through the darkest days. She regularly sent me encouraging cards, emails, gift baskets, books, prank gifts—anything to keep me afloat. And she certainly did. She never stopped doing charity work and inspiring people to be open about their own challenges. She saw clearly what her purpose was in life and made the most of it, investing her heart and soul into the work she believed in.

Brianne died on August 14, 2016, at age 36. After years of fighting, she ultimately succumbed to complications of her disease. In the time she had, she connected with countless people, overcoming the intimidation others felt through her humor and candid approach to her condition. Her directness made everyone comfortable. Many times, when I might have thought to myself, "I'm having a bad day," I'd think of Brianne and consider how she truly mastered the art of leveraging adversity and rising above her challenges. She is still perhaps the most authentic person I've ever met. In an interview with my mentor, Bill Halamandaris, Brianne said, "It's hard to stop listening when people tell you to quit. It's hard to ignore the world when it seems no one thinks you can succeed; but it gets easier. The first time you believe in yourself enough to accomplish the impossible, an inner strength is created that lasts a lifetime."

APPENDIX A

37 QUALITIES OF AN EFFECTIVE ASSISTANT CITY MANAGER, COURTESY OF INTERNATIONAL CITY/ COUNTY MANAGEMENT ASSOCIATION[6]

- Persistence
- Team player/relationship builder
- Delegate and hold others accountable
- Good role model/positive
- Flexible/adaptable
- Scout, gather, and connect
- Teamwork and relationships
- Strategic partner
- Get things done
- Trust and honesty
- Be able/willing to take on any project, task, or issue
- Know what the Manager is thinking

---

6   www.icma.org

- Run the staff
- Be present
- At times act as the filter
- Ability to "lead up"
- Tells the truth = faces the brutal facts
- Excellent communication skills
- Relationship builder
- Influence without authority
- Accept when a decision doesn't go your way
- Working with Consultants: Work hard to be their very favorite client
- Say yes with enthusiasm, say no with compassion
- Remember, it's their town (Councilmembers)
- Focus on relationships and results
- Understand your strengths and use them to develop others
- "Mind the gap"
- You have to be the person that bridges the gap between department head and manager
- Maintain work life balance
- Sense of humor
- Respect what you don't know and what stress the manager might be under
- Being a confidante
- Competent
- Go to person
- Advocate
- Interpreter

- Someone who can be the buffer between the managers and the department heads...but don't forget what level of the team they are really on

ACKNOWLEDGMENTS

I've come to understand that the greatest gift you can give to someone is to believe in them, despite their own doubts. I thank all of the following, and those unnamed, who gave me strength and confidence and kept me in pursuit of that where I found meaning.

First and foremost, to my wife Nicole, who has been at my side in this journey of pivots, always listening, supporting, and tackling life's challenges with me. I thank you for all your gifts, especially our children Leah, Clara, Ella, and Noah who keep me focused, fulfilled, and attempting to fill buckets.

Thank you to my parents, Ed and Judy, who kept me alive more than once and who have taught me so many lessons, one today rising to the top: "Life is a series of adjustments." My in-laws, Bruce and Dianne, for going along on this ride and supporting us through so many hurdles.

To my best friends since the first day of kindergarten, Dennis and Tom, for defining loyalty. To my Thunder Buddy, Darryl Polk, for your countless hours of book brainstorming, partnering, and making things better together.

To Bill and Angie Halamandaris, for your mentoring and keeping me afloat in Summer '99; Dr. Jeffrey Bone, without whose encouragement this book wouldn't have been written; Jane Atkinson, my speaker coach, for helping me build my speaking career; and Dr. Jane Goodall, for your friendship, humility, and inspiration.

Thank you to Greg Devereaux, for teaching me the nobility of public service and power of leadership; to Chris Hughes, for taking a big gamble on me and living "Successful, not Famous"; and Ben Siegel, for creating an environment where bulletproof transparency and ethics are the standard.

Honored by the men and women of the Ontario Fire Department, Ontario Police Department, and the city of Ontario, where I had the honor of serving and was professionally raised, and the entire team at the city of San Juan Capistrano, who demonstrate municipal excellence.

To all my healthcare professionals, including Dr. Diemha T. Hoang; Kim Peterson and Michelle Ranae Wild at Coastline Acquired Brain Injury Program; the team at Western University School of Health Sciences, including Dr. Elizabeth Hoppe, Dr. Valerie Quan, and Dr. Chris Chase; neuro-optometrist Dr. Eric Ikeda from Optometric Vision Care Associates Inc.; and my case manager, Debi J. Campbell, for the rescue.

And to my entire publishing team at Scribe Media, including Tucker Max, JT McCormick, Zach Obront, James Timberlake, Barbara Boyd, Erin Tyler, and Harlan Clifford. Best in the business in my humble opinion.

ABOUT THE AUTHOR

JACOB GREEN'S extensive leadership experience comes from a variety of career and life experiences. As an executive, he has managed hundreds of employees and navigated a half-billion-dollar budget. As a keynote speaker, facilitator, and coach, Jacob works with clients like Mattel, FedEx, Hyundai Capital, and many others to inspire audiences with his speeches tailored to each client.

But Jacob's life experience is even more impactful than his career achievements. Jacob took on a robber at a subway station when he was a college freshman. Not a Jiu-Jitsu practitioner, Jacob wound up getting struck in the head numerous times by the violent criminal. The good news was, his cranium kept two terrified subway workers safe!

The traumatic brain injury Jacob sustained forced him

into nearly three years of full-time rehabilitation, after which he battled back to earn his bachelor's degree, master's degree, and work his way up in a large organization as a top executive. A frequent public speaker, Jacob's clients describe his talks as "inspiring and high-energy," and say he "talked to us like an old friend."

Jacob's engaging stories come from the heart. Instead of empty catch phrases that pollute many corporate books, Jacob's authentic stories resonate with readers looking to be inspired and even challenged.

Jacob has received numerous awards for his leadership, including the National Caring Award, the Orange County Human Relations Award, and Most Inspiring Student at UC Irvine, and is the youngest recipient of the Gene Lentzner Humanitarian Award. He's just as proud to be rewarded with an embrace from an audience member who is brought to tears or given goosebumps for the first time in a while.